# Modern
# Military Aircraft

# Modern Military Aircraft

Multi-role Fighters • Interceptors • Bombers • Transports

Edward Ward

Copyright © 2025 Amber Books Ltd

Amber Books Ltd
United House
North Road
London N7 9DP
United Kingdom
www.amberbooks.co.uk
Facebook: amberbooks
YouTube: amberbooksltd
Instagram: amberbooksltd
X(Twitter): @amberbooks

All rights reserved. No part of this work may be reproduced,
stored in a retrieval system, or transmitted in any form or by
any means, electronic, mechanical, photocopying, recording,
or otherwise, without the prior permission of the copyright holder.

ISBN: 978-1-83886-608-2

Project Editor: Michael Spilling
Design: Andrew Easton & Keren Harragan
Picture Research: Terry Forshaw

Printed and bound in China

**ARTWORK CREDITS:**
All artworks courtesy Amber Books Ltd, except the following:
Anatoliy Matviyenko: 16, 19, 24–25, 42–43, 57, 73, 75, 87, 96–97, 123, 126–127, 128–129,
   132–133, 148–149, 151, 169, 176–177, 179, 194, 195
Edward Jackson (Artbyedo): 212–215
Rolando Ugolini: 14, 18, 28, 34–35, 36, 37 (lower), 38–39, 48–50, 60, 61 (lower), 62–63, 68,
   70–71, 86, 88, 90–91, 94–95, 98–99, 101, 110–111, 114–115, 118, 124, 125 (lower), 131,
   140, 155, 159, 166–168, 172–173, 180–184, 185 (top), 190–191, 198, 200–201, 208–209
Teasel Studios: 5, 17, 20–23, 30, 37 (top), 44–45, 52, 54–55, 76, 77 (lower), 78–80, 82,
   84–85, 92–93, 100, 106–107, 142, 164, 174–175, 186, 196–197, 202, 204–205, 218–219

# Contents

| | |
|---|---|
| Introduction | 6 |
| Fighter Aircraft | 10 |
| Attack, Bomber & Anti-Submarine Aircraft | 108 |
| Transport & Reconnaissance | 170 |
| Index | 220 |
| Picture Credits | 224 |

# Introduction

**Modern military airpower in the third decade of the 21st century is a mix of seeming contradictions. Most of the military aircraft flying today and included in this book first flew during the Cold War, a fact that reflects the incredible cost of developing a viable modern combat aircraft.**

Even the Lockheed Martin F-22 Raptor, generally considered the most formidable fighter plane on the planet, was flying in prototype form in 1990, before the collapse of the Soviet Union. Cost is also the driver for the ever-increasing requirement to fulfil as many roles as possible with the same aircraft.

**Multirole dominance**
Virtually all contemporary advanced training aircraft are capable of undertaking attack duties and the idea of a pure air-superiority fighter is, today, essentially unthinkable. The Lockheed Martin F-35 was intended from the outset to be a fighter and attack aircraft and even the aforementioned F-22, an air-superiority fighter through and through, has to date been used in action only to drop bombs on Syria, (and, admittedly, shoot down a balloon).

Yet even though many of the individual aircraft types may be decades old, the explosion in capability of digital technologies has seen a leap take place that shows no sign of slowing down. Bombs and missiles are routinely delivered with astounding precision, but for the aircraft that deliver them this new reality also brings threats.

**Left: A US Air Force F-35A Lightning II from the 58th Fighter Squadron, 33rd Fighter Wing, Eglin AFB, Florida, navigates towards an Air Force Reserve KC-135 Stratotanker for refueling, 2013.**

## INTRODUCTION

**Right: Major Josh Gunderson, a Lockheed Martin F-22 Demonstration Team pilot, performs during an aerial demonstration at the Singapore Airshow 2020. The F-22 Demonstration Team travels to air shows around the world to showcase the performance and capabilities of the world's premier fifth-generation fighter.**

The Russian invasion of Ukraine and the considerable numbers of aircraft losses experienced by both sides in that conflict have served to highlight how vulnerable conventional combat aircraft are to modern guided weapons, whether MANPADS (man-portable air-defence systems) or air-to-air missiles.

### Unmanned combat air vehicles

The Ukrainian conflict has also served to demonstrate the increasing importance and capability of unmanned combat air vehicles. UCAVs are sure to become ever-more dominant in future conflicts, not least in the form of 'Loyal Wingman' drones: unmanned aircraft that support, protect and supplement manned aircraft. No such UCAV is known to be operational but several are in development and are likely to dramatically alter the battlespace of the future.

## INTRODUCTION

# Fighter Aircraft

The most numerous fighters in service today, such as the General Dynamics F-16 and Sukhoi Su-27 'Flanker', were designed to excel at close-in WVR (Within Visual Range) combat, or 'dogfighting' as it is popularly known. However, air combat is increasingly dominated by sensor equipment that can detect enemy aircraft and fire missiles while in the BVR (Beyond Visual Range) realm. Today's most potent fighters are formidable in both these arenas – virtually all are multirole – and many are 'swing-role', being able to switch from air supremacy to ground attack mid-mission.

Opposite: A Russian air force Sukhoi Su-27 multirole fighter gains altitude at the international air show MAKS 2011 in Zhukovsky, Russia.

FIGHTER AIRCRAFT

# AIDC F-CK-1 Ching Kuo

> Taiwan's most advanced aircraft project to date, the Ching Kuo was intended to replace the ageing Northrop F-5 and Lockheed F-104 fighters in service.

During the 1980s, the US refrained from supplying either the General Dynamics F-16 or McDonnell Douglas F/A-18 to Taiwan, and so it was decided to develop an indigenous fighter of similar capability. Flying for the first time in May 1989, the initial F-CK-1s entered service during 1994, by which time Taiwan had managed to procure the F-16s it had wanted all along, as well as a batch of Mirage

A single-seat and a two-seat Ching Kuo conduct an emergency take-off exercise at Ching Chuan Kang Air Base near Taiwan.

### AIDC F-CK-1B Ching Kuo

**Weight (maximum take-off):** 22,487kg (27,000lb)
**Dimensions:** Length 14.48m (47ft 6in), Wingspan 9m (29ft 6in), Height 4.42m (14ft 6in)
**Powerplant:** Two 4291kg (9462lb) thrust ITEC TFE1042-70 turbofan engines
**Maximum speed:** 1275km/h (792mph)

**Range:** 1110km (689 miles)
**Ceiling:** 16,760m (55,000ft)
**Crew:** 2
**Armament:** One 20mm (0.79in) rotary six-barrel cannon; six pylons for AAMs, AASMs and various combinations of rocket or gun pods

FIGHTER AIRCRAFT

**All images:**
Twenty-eight examples of the F-CK-1B Ching Kuo two-seater were built, primarily for operational conversion and proficiency training, though this variant retains the full combat capability of the single-seater.

2000s. Ultimately only 130 production Ching Kuos were built out of the 256 originally planned, 28 of which were completed as F-CK-1B two-seaters with the rest being F-CK-1A single-seat aircraft.

## Upgrade
All aircraft in service were upgraded by 2018 to F-CK-1C standard, or -1D for two-seaters, featuring improved electronics and systems as well as provision for more fuel and a greater variety of weapons. Never offered for export, the Ching Kuo remains in frontline service in 2025.

FIGHTER AIRCRAFT

# BAE Systems Hawk

> Although designed primarily as a trainer, the Hawk was intended to have a secondary function as an air defence fighter, and a single-seat variant was also developed.

The basic design of the Hawk dates to the early 1970s and has proved a huge success, serving with some 19 nations in addition to its country of origin. First flying in 1974, over 1000 examples have been manufactured to date and although no longer built by BAE Systems, production continues today in India at HAL.

The mid 1980s saw development of a single-seater optimized for

The Royal Australian Air Force (RAAF) ordered 33 Hawk 127s in 1997, which were built under licence in Australia.

### BAE Systems Hawk 128

**Weight (maximum take-off):** 9,100kg (20,000lb)
**Dimensions:** 12.43m (40ft 9in), Wingspan: 9.94m (32ft 7in), Height: 3.98m (13ft 1in)
**Powerplant:** One Rolls-Royce Turbomeca Adour Mk. 951 turbofan rated at 29kN (6,500lbf) thrust

**Maximum speed:** 1028km/h (639mph)
**Range:** 2520km (1565 miles)
**Ceiling:** 13,565m (44,500ft)
**Crew:** 2
**Armament:** One optional 30mm (1.18in) ADEN cannon, in centreline pod; up to 3,085kg (6,800lb) of weapons on five hardpoints

FIGHTER AIRCRAFT

**Opposite:**
The Hawk 200 retains the excellent agility of its trainer forebear. This Royal Malaysian Air Force example bears the pilot's callsign 'Mongoose' on the nose.

**Above:**
Indonesia placed an order for the Hawk in 1978 and has operated the aircraft ever since.

**Above:**
The RAF 'Red Arrows' have flown the Hawk since 1979. The ventral tank contains diesel fuel, which is used to produce the team's smoke trails.

combat roles, the Hawk 200, and although this fighter variant did not emulate the export success of its progenitor, the aircraft did find a place in the inventories of Indonesia, Malaysia and Oman, continuing to serve in all three nations in the early 2020s.

## US Navy service

Further success came when the US Navy adopted the Hawk in modified form as a carrier-capable training aircraft, the T-45 Goshawk, replacing both the T-2 Buckeye and TA-4J Skyhawk, and entering service in 1991.

FIGHTER AIRCRAFT

# CAC/PAC JF-17 Thunder

**Developed to replace Pakistan's ageing fleet of Chinese A-5s and F-7s as well as older Mirage III and Vs, the multirole JF-17 was primarily designed in China.**

The deterioration of relations between the US and both China and Pakistan in the 1990s resulted in Pakistan struggling to acquire an affordable modern combat aircraft and the JF-17 was developed to supplement the F-16s it had acquired in the 1980s. As a collaboration between Pakistan and China, the new aircraft was effectively immune from US sanctions and made its maiden flight in August

Pakistan co-developed the JF-17 primarily for its own needs, but the type's capability has resulted in considerable export interest.

### CAC/PAC JF-17 Thunder

**Weight (maximum take-off):** 13,500kg (29,762lb)
**Dimensions:** Length 14.33m (47ft), Wingspan 9.44m (31ft), Height 4.57m (15ft)
**Powerplant:** One Klimov RD-93 afterburning turbofan rated at 49.4kN (11,100lbf) thrust dry, 84.4kN (19,000lbf) with afterburner

**Maximum speed:** 1910km/h (1190mph)
**Range:** 1741km (1082 miles) with drop tanks
**Ceiling:** 16,916m (55,500ft)
**Crew:** 1
**Armament:** One 23mm (0.91in) Gryazev-Shipunov GSh-23 rotary cannon; up to 3,400kg (7,500lb) fuel and ordnance on eight hardpoints

FIGHTER AIRCRAFT

**Opposite:**
Azerbaijan ordered 16 JF-17s in early 2024 to supplement its MiG-29 and Su-25 fleets, the largest order in monetary terms for military equipment that Pakistan has yet received.

**Above:**
Myanmar has taken delivery of 13 JF-17s but it has proved troublesome in service with the military junta, resulting in the entire fleet being grounded in the early 2020s.

**Above:**
Pakistan is the largest operator of the type by a considerable margin with 188 in service or on order in 2025.

2003, entering service in March of 2007. Fifty-eight per cent of the aircraft is manufactured in Pakistan and the remaining 42 per cent produced in China, with final assembly taking place in Pakistan.

## Pakistan service

Despite improving relations between the US and Pakistan allowing the export and support of further F-16s in the early 2000s, the JF-17 is the most numerous combat type in Pakistan's inventory, with 149 in service in late 2024 and further examples in production. As a relatively cheap and capable multirole aircraft, the JF-17 has proved a success on the export market with examples either ordered or delivered to Azerbaijan, Iraq, Myanmar and Nigeria.

FIGHTER AIRCRAFT

# Chengdu J-7/F-7 'Fishbed'/'Fishcan'

China's reverse-engineered MiG-21 clone differed from the original in many respects and in developed form remains in service with a dozen nations.

Although China received a few complete MiG-21s, the breakdown in relations between the USSR and China in the early 1960s resulted in vital documentation and technical information being withheld from the Chinese. Subsequently, the aircraft entered production in 1964 only as a result of reverse-engineering the Soviet originals – a process that resulted in some improvements to the

Sri Lanka maintains a small fleet of Chengdu F-7 aircraft which form the fighter component of the Sri Lanka Air Force (SLAF).

### Chengdu J-7

**Weight (maximum take-off):** 7540kg (16,623lb)
**Dimensions:** Length 14.88m (48ft 10in), Wingspan 8.32m (27ft 4in), Height 4.11m (13ft 6in)
**Powerplant:** One Liyang Wopen-13F afterburning turbojet, 44.1kN (9,900lbf) thrust dry
**Maximum speed:** 2200km/h (1400mph, 1200kn)

**Range:** 850km (530 miles)
**Ceiling:** 17,500m (57,400ft)
**Crew:** 1
**Armament:** Two 30mm (1.18in) Type 30-1 cannon, 60 rounds per gun; five hardpoints: four underwing, one centreline under-fuselage 2000kg (4,400lb) maximum; 55mm rocket pod (12 rounds), 90mm rocket pod (7 rounds)

FIGHTER AIRCRAFT

**Opposite:**
A Chengdu J-7A in People's Liberartion Army Air Force (PLAAF) markings.

**Above (both images):**
Finished here in typically anonymous air superiority grey, the J-7 has been re-assigned to the training role in the PLAAF as much more sophisticated fighter aircraft have entered the inventory.

design, notably in the fuel system and the adoption, early in the J-7's production life, of a rearward opening canopy.

## Redesign

Initial production was slow due to the Cultural Revolution but the aircraft was then manufactured continuously until 2012, with over 2000 constructed. The airframe was subject to a major redesign in the 1980s, resulting in a significant improvement in agility and the adoption of some Western electronic equipment. Widely exported (as the F-7), the J-7 still forms an important part of several air forces with China fielding the largest fleet and Myanmar, North Korea and Pakistan all boasting significant numbers of this now quite elderly fighter.

FIGHTER AIRCRAFT

# Chengdu J-10 'Firebird'

A medium-sized air superiority fighter with a distinctive canard layout, the J-10 has seen considerable evolutionary development since its appearance and has performed combat missions with Pakistan.

First flown in 1998, the J-10 entered production in 2002 and is in service with the People's Liberation Army Air Force (PLAAF) in considerable numbers, over 600 having been built by 2024 with production continuing. Early examples featured a Russian AL-31 engine, an intake with splitter plates and a pulse Doppler radar of modest capability. By contrast, the J-10C, which entered service in

This two-seat J-10S of the August 1st Aerobatic Team, demonstrating its smoke trail capability, shows off the 'letterbox' intake of earlier variants.

### Chengdu J-10B

**Weight (maximum take-off):** 20,500kg (45,195lb)
**Dimensions:** Length 16.03m (52ft 7in), Wingspan 9.25m (30ft 4in), Height 5.43m (17ft 10in)
**Powerplant:** One Saturn AL-31FN M1 turbofan engine rated at 79.43kN (17,860lb) of thrust with afterburning

**Maximum speed:** Mach 2.1
**Range:** 2250km (1400 miles)
**Ceiling:** 17,000m (56,000ft)
**Crew:** 1
**Armament:** One 23mm (0.9in) twin-barrel GSh-23 cannon plus a maximum of 6800kg (15,400lb) of disposable stores carried on 11 hardpoints

FIGHTER AIRCRAFT

**Above:**
The August 1st Aerobatic Team (named after the date of founding of the People's Liberation Army in 1927) replaced the J-7 with the J-10A in May 2009.

**Opposite & above:**
Later J-10 variants are easily identified by their distinctive diverterless supersonic intakes. In recent years a switch has been made to low-visibility national markings as seen on the example above.

2018, features the much more reliable domestically produced WS-10 engine, a diverterless supersonic intake (DSI) and a more capable AESA fire-control radar.

## Aerobatic team

As well as forming a significant part of the operational Chinese inventory, the J-10 also forms the equipment of the August 1st Aerobatic Team, appearing at a number of international air shows. The J-10C was also the first variant of the aircraft to attract an export order, with Pakistan ordering 25 J-10CEs in December 2022. These aircraft have subsequently seen action in a series of air strikes during January 2024, targeting Baloch separatist groups in Iran.

FIGHTER AIRCRAFT

# Chengdu J-20 'Fagin'

> The most advanced combat aircraft to enter squadron service in China, the J-20 is in full production and serves with the People's Liberation Army Air Force (PLAAF) in large numbers.

Although the exact capability of the J-20 remains unknown to Western observers, it is clear that this formidable aircraft represents a considerable advance on previous Chinese fighter designs. Flown for the first time in January 2011, the J-20 achieved initial operating capability during 2017 and over 300 examples of the aircraft were believed to be in service by mid 2024. There

The impressive size of the J-20's airframe allows for both a large internal weapons bay and high fuel capacity, conferring long range.

### Chengdu J-20A

**Weight (maximum take-off):** 37,013kg (81,600lb)
**Dimensions:** Length 20.4m (66ft 10in), Wingspan 13.5m (44ft 4in), Height 4.45m (14ft 7in)
**Powerplant:** Two Saturn AL-31FN turbofans each rated at 145kN (33,000lb) thrust with afterburning
**Maximum speed:** Mach 2.0+
**Range:** 3400km (2113 miles)

**Ceiling:** 20,000m (65,617ft)
**Crew:** 1
**Armament:** Disposable ordnance carried in one large weapon bay in the lower fuselage, typically comprising up to four PL-15 AAMs, plus two PL-10 AAMs carried in lateral weapon bays behind the intakes; optional additional ordnance on four underwing pylons

FIGHTER AIRCRAFT

**Above:**
This J-20A, involved in flight testing, was assigned to the 176th Air Brigade, based at Dingxin Air Base in the Gobi desert.

**Opposite top:**
Serving with the PLAAF's 172nd Air Brigade, this J-20A was utilized in the flight test and training role at Gangzhou.

**Right:** J-20 stealth fighter jets perform during the 14th China International Aviation and Aerospace Exhibition, or Airshow China 2022.

is some debate as to whether the aircraft can be considered truly 'stealthy' by contemporary US standards but the airframe does make use of several technologies, such as internal weapons bays and diverterless intakes, and the design has been improved in this regard over its production life to date, perhaps most notably gaining serrated afterburner nozzles for its WS-10 engines.

## Air superiority fighter

As an air superiority fighter, the J-20 has been described as possessing comparable manoeuvrability to the Chengdu J-10, while demonstrating superior low observability. It is believed to be superior to the Sukhoi Su-57, becoming the first Chinese combat aircraft to demonstrate superior capability to a direct Russian equivalent and making plain the enormous strides that have recently been made by the Chinese aviation industry.

FIGHTER AIRCRAFT

# Dassault Mirage III and Mirage 5

> A classic Cold War design flown by over 20 nations, the delta-wing Mirage proved staggeringly successful but is now reaching the end of its operational career.

Dassault utilized the delta-wing format for a lightweight fighter it flew in the mid 1950s and named the Mirage but it was decided a larger aircraft, the Mirage II, would be more useful. Neither of these designs entered production, but an engine change to the promising new SNECMA Atar resulted in the Mirage III, which was built in large numbers, including under licence in Australia and Switzerland.

Australia built 116 Mirages under licence for the RAAF, including 16 examples of the two-seat Mirage IIID pictured here.

## Dassault Mirage 5F

**Weight (maximum take-off):** 13,700kg (30,203lb)
**Dimensions:** Length 15.55m (51ft 0in), Wingspan 8.22m (27ft 0in), Height 4.5m (14ft 9in)
**Powerplant:** One SNECMA Atar 9C afterburning turbojet, rated at 41.97kN (9,440lbf) thrust dry, 60.8kN (13,700lbf) with afterburner

**Maximum speed:** 2350km/h (1460mph)
**Range:** 1250km (780 miles)
**Ceiling:** 18,000m (59,000ft)
**Crew:** 1
**Armament:** Two 30mm (1.18in) DEFA 552 cannons; up to 4,000kg (8,800lb) of ordnance and fuel on five hardpoints

# FIGHTER AIRCRAFT

**Opposite:**
South Africa operated Mirages for several years and used its fleet in combat in the South African Border Wars with Angola, Namibia and Zaire.

**Both images:**
Libya was one of the largest Mirage 5 operators, taking delivery of 110 examples of the French delta fighter. By 2008 all had been withdrawn and sold to Pakistan as a source of spare parts.

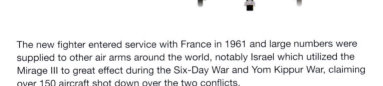

The new fighter entered service with France in 1961 and large numbers were supplied to other air arms around the world, notably Israel which utilized the Mirage III to great effect during the Six-Day War and Yom Kippur War, claiming over 150 aircraft shot down over the two conflicts.

## Mirage 5

Israeli requirements resulted in the development of the Mirage 5, externally very similar to the Mirage III but recognizable by its extended nose. The Mirage 5 was also a great export success with large fleets operated by Belgium, Egypt, Libya and Pakistan. The latter nation continues to operate a combined total of around 150 Mirage III and Mirage 5s in 2025, though the aircraft is expected to be replaced in the near future.

FIGHTER AIRCRAFT

# Dassault Mirage F1

Although long retired by its country of origin, the Mirage F1 soldiers on in the inventories of several nations and, somewhat surprisingly, with several private contractors.

The Mirage F1 had a long developmental period. Flown for the first time in 1966, it was initially viewed as little more than a back-up to the more advanced Mirage F2 but entered production and service in 1974 following the F2's cancellation. Widely exported, the F1 has seen much combat service over the last five decades, notably during the Iran–Iraq War in which an Iraqi Mirage F1 shot

Spain operated Mirage F1s between 1975 and 2013, serving as the nation's premier air defence interceptors until superseded by the F/A-18 Hornet.

### Dassault Mirage F1

**Weight (maximum take-off):** 16,200kg (35,715lb)
**Dimensions:** Length 5.3m (50ft 2in), Wingspan 8.4m (27ft 7in), Height 4.5m (14ft 9in)
**Powerplant:** One SNECMA Atar 9K-50 afterburning turbojet engine, rated at 49.03kN (11,020lbf) thrust dry, 70.6kN (15,900lbf) with afterburner

**Maximum speed:** 2338km/h (1453mph)
**Range:** 3300km (2100 miles) with maximum external fuel
**Ceiling:** 20,000m (66,000ft)
**Crew:** 1
**Armament:** One 30mm (1.18in) DEFA 553 cannon; up to 6,300kg (13,900lb) of ordnance or fuel on seven hardpoints

# FIGHTER AIRCRAFT

**All images:**
South Africa operated both the Mirage F1CZ and F1AZ. 48 aircraft were procured for the South African Air Force (SAAF) and these saw considerable action during the long-running South African Border Wars. The original order for 100 aircraft was cut short by an arms embargo.

down an Iranian F-14 Tomcat. Today it remains operational with five nations of which Morocco is the largest user with 27 aircraft.

## Private service

However, the private ATAC company in the US acquired 63 former French Mirage F1s for use in dissimilar air combat training and for aggressor squadrons under contract to the US military, a role also undertaken by the 20 ex-Spanish private Mirage F1s of Draken International. ATAC intends to maintain around 30 to 45 F1 airframes in airworthy condition, the largest Mirage F1 fleet in the world.

27

FIGHTER AIRCRAFT

# Dassault Mirage 2000

Designed as an air superiority fighter to replace the Mirage III, the Mirage 2000 was subsequently developed into numerous variants to fulfil a wide range of roles.

The first Mirage 2000 flew on 10 March 1978 and a two-seat version, the Mirage 2000B, followed it into the air in October 1980. The first unit to become operational with the Mirage 2000C-1 was Escadre de Chasse 1/2 'Cigognes' in 1984.

The Mirage 2000N was armed with the ASMP medium-range nuclear missile and while this variant has now retired, the conventionally armed

This Armee de l'Air two-seat Mirage 2000 was photographed conducting a combat patrol over Afghanistan in December 2008.

### Dassault Mirage 2000C

**Weight (maximum take-off):** 17,000kg (37,479lb)
**Dimensions:** Length 14.36m (47ft 1in), Wingspan 9.13m (29ft 11in), Height 5.2m (17ft 1in)
**Powerplant:** One SNECMA M53-P2 turbofan engine, rated at 64.3kN (14,500lbf) thrust dry, 95.1kN (21,400lbf) with afterburner

**Maximum speed:** Mach 2.2, 2336km/h (1452mph)
**Range:** 1550km (960 miles)
**Ceiling:** 17,060m (55,970ft)
**Crew:** 1
**Armament:** Two 30mm (1.2in) DEFA 554 revolver cannon; up to 6,300kg (13,900lb) of external fuel and ordnance on nine hardpoints

FIGHTER AIRCRAFT

**Opposite:**
The Mirage 2000 formed the backbone of the French Air Force during the last two decades of the 20th century. This example was on the strength of Escadron de Chasse 1/2 'Les Cigognes'.

**Both images:**
The Mirage 2000P remains the most numerous fighter of the Peruvian Air Force, though replacements for the ageing aircraft were actively being sought in 2025. The Mirage 2000 fleet is operated by Escuadrón de Caza 412 based at La Joya.

Mirage 2000D two-seat attack derivative remains in service in France. The Mirage 2000 was also exported in large numbers, and in 2024 remains in service with Egypt, Greece, India, Peru, Taiwan and the UAE. In Indian Air Force service, the aircraft, designated Mirage 2000H, is known as the *Vajra* (Thunderstreak).

## Active service

The agile Mirage 2000 has seen considerable operational service since its combat debut during the Gulf War in 1990, mostly in the strike role. In March 2024, however, two Mirage 2000s scored the first French air-to-air victories since World War II when they shot down two Houthi drones over the Red Sea.

FIGHTER AIRCRAFT

# Dassault Rafale

> A contemporary of the Eurofighter Typhoon, the Rafale is also a canard layout twin engine of similar performance and a highly capable multirole combat aircraft.

Utilized by the French Air Force and Navy, the Rafale owes its existence to France's withdrawal from the 'Future European Fighter Aircraft' programme, which would eventually become the Typhoon, to focus on a domestically produced aircraft. Dassault subsequently produced a technology demonstrator in 1986 with a genuine Rafale prototype flying in 1991. Subsequent budget reductions

This Rafale of Escadron de Chasse 1/7 'Provence' received striking markings for the annual NATO 'Tiger Meet' exercises.

### Dassault Rafale C

**Weight (maximum take-off):** 24,500kg (54,013lb)
**Dimensions:** Length 15.27m (50ft 1in), Wingspan 10.90m (35ft 9in), Height 5.34m (17ft 6in)
**Powerplant:** Two Snecma M88-4e turbofans, rated at 50.04kN (11,250lbf) thrust each dry, 75kN (17,000lbf) with afterburner

**Maximum speed:** Mach 1.8, 1912km/h (1188mph)
**Range:** 1850km (1150 miles)
**Ceiling:** 15,835m (51,952ft)
**Crew:** 1
**Armament:** One fixed 30mm (1.2in) GIAT 30/M79; up to 9,500kg (20,900lb) of stores on 14 hardpoints

FIGHTER AIRCRAFT

**Opposite:**
This Rafale M with distinctive low-vis national markings is based at Landivisiau Air Base when it is not serving aboard the carrier *Charles De Gaulle*.

**Both images:**
Rafale M01 was the first naval Rafale, and was heavily employed in trials work. Initially this took place in the US at NAS Lakehurst in New Jersey before moving well aboard the French Navy aircraft carrier *Foch*.

following the end of the Cold War saw service entry delayed but the Rafale has been operational since 2001, initially with the Navy.

## Two-seater variant

The most important variants to be produced are the Rafale B two-seater, the Rafale C single-seat air superiority fighter of the Air Force, and the Rafale M naval variant, featuring arrester hook and strengthened landing gear, fully compatible with operating from US carriers. French Rafales have subsequently served in action over Iraq, Libya, Afghanistan, Mali and Syria.

The Rafale has also proved successful on the export market with five international operators currently flying the aircraft and three further nations having placed orders for the type. The most important non-French Rafale user is India with 36 aircraft in service with the Air Force and a further 26 on order for carrier use with the Indian Navy.

FIGHTER AIRCRAFT

# Eurofighter Typhoon

Fast, agile and powerful, the Typhoon is probably Western Europe's most formidable multirole combat aircraft, providing the fighter backbone of five European nations.

The multinational Typhoon provides the backbone of Germany, Italy, Spain and the UK, the nations which partnered to develop and manufacture it, though the aircraft bears a striking resemblance to the British Aerospace EAP (Experimental Aircraft Programme) which had flown in 1986. The Typhoon's first flight took place in 1994 but political and funding issues delayed development, resulting in the

Luftwaffe two-seat EF2000(T) in flight with an unusually heavy payload of fuel tanks, Paveways and IRIS-T air-to-air missiles.

### Eurofighter Typhoon

**Weight (maximum take-off):** 23,500kg (51,809lb)
**Dimensions:** Length 15.96m (52ft 4in), Wingspan 10.95m (35ft 11in), Height 5.28m (17ft 4in)
**Powerplant:** Two Eurojet EJ200 turbofan engines, each rated at 60kN (13,500lbf) thrust dry, 90kN (20,200lbf) with afterburner

**Maximum speed:** Mach 2.35, 2500km/h (1600mph)
**Range:** 2900km (1800 miles)
**Ceiling:** 16,764m (55,000ft)
**Crew:** 1
**Armament:** One fixed 27mm (1in) Mauser BK-27 cannon; up to 9,000kg (19,800lb) of stores on 13 hardpoints

# FIGHTER AImport

**All images:**
The seventh development airframe, ZH588 was employed in trials work after its first flight in April 1994. This aircraft was retired in 2007 and is currently displayed in the RAF Museum, Hendon.

first production aircraft only being delivered in 2003. The aircraft was intended to be a 'swing role' platform, able to fulfil more than one task in the same mission, and since entering service the aircraft has proved itself in a variety of roles.

### 'Swing role' platform

German and British aircraft have used the aircraft's impressive rate of climb to advantage to intercept Russian Tu-95s approaching national airspace while Royal Air Force (RAF) Typhoons have attacked ground targets in Libya and Syria, and Saudi Arabian Eurofighters have spearheaded the controversial bombing campaign in Yemen. As well as Saudi Arabia, Austria, Kuwait, Oman and Qatar have all acquired Typhoons, though comparatively few export orders have been placed for the aircraft to date. The most recent production aircraft are being constructed for the Luftwaffe to 'Tranche 4' standard featuring the latest CAPTOR E AESA radar.

FIGHTER AIRCRAFT

# General Dynamics F-16A/B Fighting Falcon

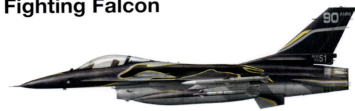

> The most successful US fighter aircraft of the last 50 years, the F-16 was developed as a lightweight, low-cost aircraft and has become, numerically, the most important fighter in the Western alliance.

US experience in Vietnam where apparently more advanced aircraft, such as the F-4 Phantom, suffered losses to seemingly obsolescent small and simple fighters, such as the MiG-17, served to suggest that there was still a place for the agile close-in dogfighter in the modern air force. The US Air Force's LWF (Lightweight Fighter) programme sought to acquire such an aircraft and the YF-16 proved

The LF tailcode denotes that this F-16B of the 56th Fighter Wing was based at Luke Air Force Base in Arizona.

### F-16A Block 15B ADF

**Weight (maximum take-off):** 17,009kg (37,500lbs)
**Dimensions:** Length 15.01m (49ft 3.5in), Wingspan 9.995m (32ft 9.5in), Height 5.09m (16ft 8.5in)
**Powerplant:** One Pratt & Whitney F100-PW-220 turbofan rated at 55.2kN (12,410lbf) dry, 106.4kN (23,930lbf) with afterburner

**Maximum speed:** Mach 2.05, 2530km/h (1570mph)
**Range:** 3862km (2400 miles)
**Ceiling:** 16,764m (55,000ft)
**Crew:** 1
**Armament:** One M61A1 20mm (0.79in) cannon; six hardpoints: AIM-9 Sidewinder, AIM-7 Sparrow, AIM-120 AMRAAM

FIGHTER AIRCRAFT

**All images:**
Resplendent in a scheme to celebrate the 90th anniversary of the 23rd Gruppo of the Italian Air Force in 2008, this aircraft was one of 34 F-16As leased by Italy pending delivery of the Eurofighter Typhoon.

the winner, beating Northrop's YF-17 (later to evolve into the successful F/A-18) in a competitive fly-off.

### 'Fighting Falcon'

The initial variant, the F-16A, was accepted into the USAF in 1979 and the official name of 'Fighting Falcon' was conferred upon it the following year, though the unofficial nickname 'Viper' would become ubiquitous. F-16 production is split into subtypes that are identified by 'Block' numbers and the F-16A incorporated Blocks 1, 5, 10, 15 and 20. Block 15 introduced the first significant change to the airframe, featuring larger stabilizers. A two-seat variant, the F-16B, broadly identical apart from the second seat, was produced concurrently with the F-16A, and 983 of these first-generation F-16s were built. The F-16A/B was very widely exported with major users including Israel and Turkey as well as a swathe of other nations.

FIGHTER AIRCRAFT

# General Dynamics F-16C/D Fighting Falcon

The single-seat F-16C was an altogether more capable warplane than the F-16A/B and together with the two-seat F-16D transformed the aircraft into a truly multirole fighter.

True to its origin as a simple lightweight fighter, although the first-generation F-16 could carry unguided bombs and rockets, it was essentially limited to a daylight air defence role. The F-16C introduced the Westinghouse AN/APG-68 multimode system radar which could provide increased range, enhanced resolution and a wider selection of operating modes. The new radar was

The F-16 is noted for the exceptional visibility conferred by its one piece canopy, seen here opened at Little Rock Air Force Base in 2014.

### F-16C Block 52

**Weight (maximum take-off):** 19,187kg (42,300lb)
**Dimensions:** Length 15.06m (49ft 5in), Wingspan 9.96m (32ft 8in), Height 4.9m (16ft)
**Powerplant:** One Pratt & Whitney F100-PW-229 turbofan rated at 131.5kN (29,560lb) with afterburning
**Maximum speed:** Mach 2.05, 2530km/h (1570mph)
**Range:** 4217km (2620 miles), with drop tanks
**Ceiling:** 18,288m (60,000ft)
**Crew:** 1
**Armament:** One 20mm (0.787in) M61A1 six-barrel rotary cannon, plus up to 7700kg (17,000lb) of disposable stores carried on nine hardpoints

FIGHTER AIRCRAFT

**Below:**
Another commemorative scheme was applied to this F-16C in 2021, in this case to honour WWII and Vietnam War ace Robin Olds.

**Opposite:**
Painted in a special scheme for the US Air Force's 50th anniversary to honour the black pilots known as the 'Tuskegee Airmen', this F-16C was serving with the 302 FS in 1997.

**Above:**
The X-62A VISTA is a one-off derivative of the F-16D which can be trimmed to mimic the handling of other aircraft and is used by the US Test Pilots School.

also compatible with more capable weapons, including the AIM-120 AMRAAM conferring a beyond-visual-range (BVR) capability on the Viper for the first time as well as allowing it to utilize guided air-to-ground missiles.

## Enlarged base

F-16C/D aircraft can be distinguished by an enlarged base for the vertical tail, forming a distinctive boxy fairing at the bottom of the fin. The F-16C entered production in 1984 and was in service in large numbers by the time of Operation Desert Storm, the first Gulf War, during which F-16s flew 13,340 sorties, the most of any aircraft type. The F-16C/Ds were gradually improved over their production life, with the mass produced and widely exported Block 50/52 aircraft becoming a benchmark of sorts. Large numbers of these mid-production F-16s remain in service worldwide.

FIGHTER AIRCRAFT

# General Dynamics/Lockheed Martin F-16E/F Desert Falcon and F-16V Viper

> The F-16 remains in production and continues to be updated. Older models are also progressively upgraded to new production standards, the most recent being the Block 70/72 F-16V.

The Block 60 F-16 was developed to meet an order from the United Arab Emirates (UAE), emerging as the F-16E in single-seat form and F-16F with a second crew member, collectively known as the Desert Falcon. A step beyond Block 50, the F-16E/F retains the conformal fuel tanks developed for use on Israeli F-16Ds, providing a significant increase in range without compromising external stores.

The conformal fuel tanks on the fuselage sides are evident on this Jordanian F-16E, completely changing the F-16's previously slim profile.

### F-16D(V) Block 70

**Weight (maximum take-off):** 20,865kg (46,000lbs)
**Dimensions:** Length 15.02m (49ft 3in), Wingspan 9.449m (31ft), Height 5.09m (16ft 8.5in)
**Powerplant:** One Pratt and Whitney F100-PW-200/220/229 or General Electric F110-GE-100/129

**Maximum speed:** Mach 2, 2470km/h (1535mph)
**Range:** 3218km (2000 miles)
**Ceiling:** 18,288m (60,000ft)
**Crew:** 2
**Armament:** One M61A1 20mm (0.787in) cannon; up to six under-wing hardpoints, three fuselage hardpoints, two wingtip pylons

FIGHTER AIRCRAFT

**Opposite:**
The Royal Bahraini Air Force operates this F-16V two-seater. In 2023, Bahrain became the first F-16 operator to take delivery of Block 70 aircraft.

**Above (both images):**
The Royal Jordanian Air Force is taking delivery of both single-seat (top) and two-seat (above lower) block 70/72 aircraft. The acquisition has proved controversial due to the exceptionally high price charged for these aircraft.

## Desert Falcon

The Desert Falcon incorporates a Northrop Grumman AN/APG-80 Multi-mode Active Electronically Scanned Array (AESA) agile-beam radar, claimed to deliver a range around three times greater than that of a US Air Force F-16C. The most formidable F-16 produced to date, however, is the F-16V, which finally rendered the 'Viper' name official and was unveiled at the 2012 Singapore Airshow.
It features an improved AN/APG-83 radar, upgraded mission computer and improvements to the cockpit offering commonality with the radar hardware and software of the F-22 and F-35. The F-16V is being offered as a new production machine or as an upgrade to earlier models, and sizeable orders for new F-16Vs have been placed by Bulgaria, Slovakia, Taiwan and Turkey. The first new-build F-16V was delivered to Bahrain in 2023.

FIGHTER AIRCRAFT

# Grumman F-14 Tomcat

> Despite its highly publicized service with the US Navy, the powerful F-14 was exported to only one nation, Iran, which continues to operate the Grumman fighter in the 2020s.

Grumman's replacement for the F-4 Phantom, the Tomcat was developed with the benefit of air combat experience gained during the Vietnam war and flew for the first time in December 1970, entering service in mid 1974. For many years the F-14 was the US Navy's primary maritime air superiority fighter and tactical reconnaissance platform until its retirement in 2006. During this period

This F-14D of VF-31 was pictured during refuelling over the Persian Gulf in 2005. Within a year all US F-14s had been retired.

### Grumman F-14A

**Weight (maximum take-off):** 33,724kg (74,348lb)
**Dimensions:** Length 19.10m (62ft 8in), Wingspan 19.45m (64ft 1.5in) wings spread, Height 4.88m (16ft 0in)
**Powerplant:** Two Pratt & Whitney TF30-P-412 afterburning turbofans, each rated at 92.97kN (20,900lb) with afterburner

**Maximum speed:** 2485km/h (1544mph) 'clean' at high altitude
**Range:** 1233km (766 miles)
**Service ceiling:** More than 15,240m (50,000ft)
**Crew:** 2
**Armament:** One 20mm (0.79in) rotary cannon; up to 6577kg (14,500lb) of external ordnance

# FIGHTER AIRCRAFT

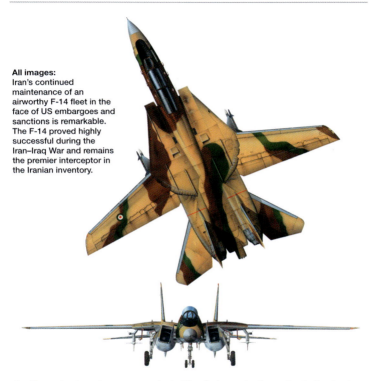

**All images:**
Iran's continued maintenance of an airworthy F-14 fleet in the face of US embargoes and sanctions is remarkable. The F-14 proved highly successful during the Iran–Iraq War and remains the premier interceptor in the Iranian inventory.

the Tomcat enjoyed an unprecedented level of popular fame due to its starring role in the 1986 film *Top Gun*.

## Iranian service

Its success on the screen was not repeated on the export market, however, and despite strenuous efforts to sell the aircraft to Canada, Germany and Japan, only Iran would take delivery of the F-14, ordering 80 aircraft in 1976. The first F-14 'kill' was scored by an Iranian aircraft in 1980, when an Iraqi Mil Mi-25 was downed, the first of at least 50 Tomcat victories scored during the Iran–Iraq War. Today, an unconfirmed number of F-14s remain operational with Iran.

FIGHTER AIRCRAFT

# Guizhou JL-9

China's JL-9 trainer and light attack aircraft mates a 21st-century wing and glass cockpit to the rear fuselage and tail surfaces of the veteran MiG-21.

Intended primarily as a training aircraft for the People's Liberation Army Air Force (PLAAF), the JL-9 has been operating with Chinese forces since October 2015, having flown for the first time in late 2003. The aircraft had originally been developed by Guizhou as the FTC-2000, a comparatively inexpensive trainer for crews of fourth-generation fighters. The FTC-2000 has also been offered on the export

The FTC-2000G is the two-seat lead-in trainer/light combat derivative of the JL-9, seen here displaying at the Zhuhai Airshow in 2018.

### Guizhou JL-9

**Weight (maximum take-off):** 9850kg (21,716lb)
**Dimensions:** Length 14.55m (47ft 9in), Wingspan 8.32m (27ft 4in), Height 4.1m (13ft 5in)
**Powerplant:** One 53.89kN (12,110lbf) thrust dry (76.53kN (17,200lbf) with afterburner) WP-14C Kunlun-3 turbojet engine

**Maximum speed:** 1480km/h (920mph)
**Range:** 2500km (1553 miles) with maximum external fuel
**Ceiling:** 16,000m (52,490ft)
**Crew:** 2
**Armament:** One 23mm (0.9in) machine gun fixed, forward firing in forward fuselage, five hardpoints for external stores

# FIGHTER AIRCRAFT

**Opposite:**
The JL-9 has been serving in small numbers as an advanced trainer with the PLAAF since 2014.

**Above (both images):**
The Guizhou JL-9G was developed as a carrier landing trainer and first flew in 2009, appearing in this attractive scheme at that year's Dubai Airshow.

market as a very cheap supersonic fighter and light attack aircraft intended to replace ageing MiG-21 and J-7 fleets, and so far has attracted orders from Sudan and Myanmar. The latter nation has taken delivery of 12 examples to date of the heavier and more heavily armed FTC-2000G export variant featuring a diverterless supersonic intake and seven hardpoints.

## Burma wars

These aircraft have been in action against Kachin Independence Army forces in the ongoing Myanmar civil war and one example was lost to an FN-6 man portable air defence system missile in January 2024.

FIGHTER AIRCRAFT

# Hal Tejas

> Currently the world's smallest and lightest aircraft in its class, the supersonic, delta-winged Tejas ('Radiance') was intended to replace the long-serving MiG-21 in IAF service.

The Tejas resulted from a 1980s programme to develop a new lightweight fighter, primarily to replace the MiG-21 as well as other types. Various developmental and political issues, not least several embargoes on both hardware and consultancy imposed by other nations, saw progress delayed for several years until the type made its first flight in January 2001. Flight testing and

An Indian Air Force Tejas with smoke dispensers for display purposes. The Tejas is a small aircraft with some excellent systems, including the Israeli Elbit Dash IV helmet.

## HAL Tejas Mark IA

**Weight (maximum take-off):** 13,500kg (29,762lb)
**Dimensions:** Length 13.2m (43ft 4in), Wingspan 8.2m (26ft 11in), Height 4.4m (14ft 5in)
**Powerplant:** One General Electric F404-GE-IN20 turbofan rated at 85kN (19,000lbf) thrust
**Maximum speed:** Mach 1.8, 2220km/h (1380mph)

**Range:** 739km (459 miles)
**Ceiling:** 16,000m (52,500ft)
**Crew:** 1
**Armament:** One fixed 23mm (0.9in) twin-barrel GSh-23 cannon, up to 5300kg (11,685lb) of stores on nine hardpoints including bombs, rockets, air-to-air and air-to-surface guided missiles

FIGHTER AIRCRAFT

**Opposite & below:**
Indian Air Force Tejas fighters.
As of 2025, India is the sole
operator of the aircraft.

**Right: The most
unusual feature
of the Tejas is the
wing, which like
the Swedish Viggen
is a delta that
combines an inner
section of moderate
sweep with a more
sharply swept outer
section.**

further development was slow as various revisions were made to the aircraft which had evolved from a pure fighter into a multirole aircraft, but the first examples entered Air Force service in 2011 with the first squadron becoming operational in 2016. The improved Mark IA is expected to enter operational service during 2025.

## Tejas Mk II
Since then, development of the more versatile medium-weight Tejas Mark II, featuring a canard design and more powerful engine, has been ongoing. Expected to fly during 2025, the Tejas Mark II is intended to equip 12 squadrons of the Indian Air Force and benefits from increased payload-carrying capacity as well as a greater internal fuel capacity, more external hardpoints, a completely redesigned cockpit and an IRST system, in addition to the existing AESA radar.

FIGHTER AIRCRAFT

# IAI Kfir

> Developed to circumvent a French arms embargo, the Kfir served only briefly as an air superiority fighter in Israel before switching to the fighter bomber role.

Israel was an enthusiastic operator of the Mirage III during the 1960s but with no availability of new aircraft or spares after 1967 the decision was taken to manufacture an unlicensed Mirage copy called the Nesher. Further development resulted in the Kfir, in which the Mirage's Atar turbojet was replaced by the more powerful General Electric J79, necessitating a major redesign of the rear fuselage

The Kfir was well liked by the pilots who flew it for Israel. The Kfir is easily identified by the distinctive air intake at the base of its tailfin.

## IAI Kfir C.2

**Weight (maximum take-off):** 16,200kg (35,721lb)
**Dimensions:** Length 15.65m (51ft 4in), Wingspan 8.22m (26ft 11.5in), Height 4.55m (14ft 11in)
**Powerplant:** One General Electric J79-J1E turbojet rated at 8119kg (17,900lb) thrust with afterburner

**Maximum speed:** 2445km/h (1520mph)
**Range:** 1000km (620 miles)
**Ceiling:** 7680m (58,000ft)
**Crew:** 1
**Armament:** One 30mm (1.19in) cannon; nine external hardpoints with provision for up to 5775kg (12,732lb) of ordnance

# FIGHTER AIRCRAFT

**All images:**
A Kfir operated by the Ecuadorian Air Force (FAE – Fuerza Aérea Ecuatoriana). It is armed with Israeli Shafrir 2 infrared-guided missiles.

and resulting in the addition of the prominent air intake at the base of the tailfin. The Kfir entered Israeli service in 1975 but was replaced in the air superiority role by the F-15 the following year, and the aircraft subsequently served until the 1990s as fighter bombers.

### In service

In 2025 the aircraft remains in service in Colombia and Sri Lanka, and the civilian contractor ATAC operates six Kfirs to provide airborne tactical training, threat simulation and research & development for the US military. The Kfir was earlier utilized in this role by the US Air Force when it was designated the F-21.

FIGHTER AIRCRAFT

# KAI T-50 Golden Eagle

> Although developed as an advanced trainer and light combat aircraft, South Korea's T-50 is increasingly being utilized as an air superiority asset both domestically and abroad.

The supersonic T-50 made its first flight in August 2002 and entered South Korean service in early 2005, initially as a lead-in trainer for Korea's F-16 and F-15 fleet. The basic design has subsequently been used as the basis for the more potent TA-50 variant, optimized for the light attack role, though still capable of operating as an advanced trainer. Specialized RA-50 and EA-50 variants have also

Indonesian Air Force T-50i Golden Eagles taxi back to the ramp at Halim Perdanakusuma Air Force Base.

### KAI FA-50 Fighting Eagle

**Weight (maximum take-off):** 12,215kg (26,929lb)
**Dimensions:** Length 13.14m (43ft 1in), Wingspan 9.45m (31ft 0in), Height 4.82m (15ft 8in)
**Powerplant:** One General Electric F404-GE-102 afterburning turbofan engine, rated at 53.07kN (11,930lbf) thrust dry, 78.7kN (17,700lbf) with afterburner
**Maximum speed:** 1838km/h (1142mph)
**Range:** 1851km (1150 miles)
**Ceiling:** 14,630m (48,000ft)
**Crew:** 1 or 2
**Armament:** General Dynamics M197 20mm (0.787in) 3-barrel rotary cannon; up to 5400kg (12,000lb) of ordnance

FIGHTER AIRCRAFT

**Opposite:**
The KAI T-50TH variant is operated by the Royal Thai Air Force.

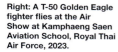

**Above:**
An Indonesian Air Force KAI T-50i Golden Eagle. The TT tailcode stands for Tempur Taktis (tactical fighter), the aircraft's role with the Indonesian forces.

**Right: A T-50 Golden Eagle fighter flies at the Air Show at Kamphaeng Saen Aviation School, Royal Thai Air Force, 2023.**

been produced for the reconnaissance and electronic warfare roles respectively. Further development resulted in the appearance of the more formidable FA-50 Fighting Eagle that features more internal fuel capacity, enhanced avionics, a tactical datalink and a longer radome containing a Korean modified Israeli EL/M-2032 pulse-Doppler radar.

## Export success

The T-50's combination of capability and keen price has seen the aircraft receive ready acceptance on the export market with five foreign nations having taken delivery of the type and a sixth, Poland, having ordered 48 examples to replace the MiG-29 and Su-22. To date, only the Philippines has utilized the TA-50 in combat, conducting strikes against various terrorist groups. As of 2025 a single-seat variant, the F-50, is under development, intended as an alternative to the F-16. Korea Aerospace Industries (KAI) claims it provides approximately 80% of the capability of the American aircraft at a significantly lower cost.

49

FIGHTER AIRCRAFT

# Lockheed Martin F-22 Raptor

> The F-22 remains the premier air superiority asset of the US Air Force (USAF), and is still generally considered the most effective fighter aircraft on the planet some 20 years after entering service.

The F-22 derives from the YF-22, the winner of an evaluation process against the rival Northrop YF-23 during the early 1990s. Although sharing the same basic configuration as the earlier test aircraft, the F-22 as it emerged featured a reworked forward fuselage allowing for a more effective radome shape and providing better visibility for the pilot. The programme as a whole was hugely expensive and suffered

Two USAF F-22 Raptors. The cockpit canopies look gold due to a metallic indium tin oxide coating to reflect radar waves.

### Lockheed Martin F-22 Raptor

**Weight (maximum take-off):** 38,000kg (83,500lb)
**Dimensions:** Length 18.9m (62ft 1in), Wingspan 13.6m (44ft 6in), Height 5.1m (16ft 8in)
**Powerplant:** Two Pratt & Whitney F119-PW-100 afterburning turbofans, each rated at 155.69kN (35,000lb) in afterburner

**Maximum speed (estimated):** 2410km/h (1500mph)
**Range:** 2977km (1850 miles)
**Ceiling:** 15,240m (50,000ft)
**Crew:** 1
**Armament:** One 20mm (0.79in) rotary cannon, plus two AIM-9 AAMs and six AIM-120 AAMs, or (ground attack) two GBU-32 JDAMs

# FIGHTER AIRCRAFT

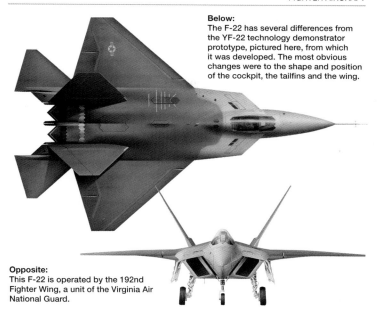

**Below:**
The F-22 has several differences from the YF-22 technology demonstrator prototype, pictured here, from which it was developed. The most obvious changes were to the shape and position of the cockpit, the tailfins and the wing.

**Opposite:**
This F-22 is operated by the 192nd Fighter Wing, a unit of the Virginia Air National Guard.

from a protracted development period and teething troubles. These, combined with budgetary concerns, especially in the aftermath of the end of the Cold War, saw procurement decrease from a planned 750 aircraft to 187 operational aircraft, delivered between 2002 and 2012, and development of two-seat and naval variants was abandoned. First use of the aircraft on combat sorties took place in 2014 when F-22s were used to attack Islamic State (ISIL) positions in Syria. To date the F-22 has achieved one air-to-air 'kill': a suspected Chinese spy balloon was destroyed in 2023.

## Supreme model

Despite its prolonged development and comparative rarity, the Raptor has matured into an exceptional combat aircraft with no credible rival worldwide until comparatively recently. The capabilities of the recently developed Su-57 and China's J-20 and new J-35 stealth fighters are not fully known and may threaten the F-22's dominance in some areas.

FIGHTER AIRCRAFT

# Lockheed Martin F-35A Lightning II

The most costly acquisition programme in history, expected to exceed two trillion dollars over its lifetime, the F-35 has overcome a lengthy development period to mature into an effective combat aircraft.

A multirole stealthy and supersonic strike fighter, the F-35 derives from the X-35 which won the Joint Strike Fighter (JSF) competition in 2001 and was primarily intended to replace the F-16, F/A-18 and AV-8B Harrier in US service. Although US led, the development of the JSF and subsequent F-35 has always been a multinational effort, initially with the United Kingdom as the single other

US Air Force Capt. Kristin Wolfe, an F-35A demonstration team pilot, performs the 'dedication pass' manoeuvre, June 2020.

### Lockheed Martin F-35A

**Weight (maximum take-off):** 31,750kg (70,000lb)
**Dimensions:** Length 15.7m (51ft 5in), Wingspan 10.7m (35ft 0in), Height 4.38m (14ft 5in)
**Powerplant:** One Pratt & Whitney F135-PW-100 afterburning turbofan rated at 178kN (40,000lb) in afterburner

**Maximum speed:** 1931km/h (1200mph)
**Range:** 2200km (1367 miles)
**Ceiling:** 15,000m (50,000ft)
**Crew:** 1
**Armament:** One 25mm (0.98in) rotary cannon, up to two AIM-120C AAMs, two 907kg (2000lb) GBU-31 JDAMs in weapons bay

FIGHTER AIRCRAFT

**Below (both images):**
The OT tailcode denotes this F-35A was on the strength of the USAF 422d Test and Evaluation Squadron at Eglin Air Force Base, Florida.

**Opposite:**
Denmark has ordered 27 F-35As for the Flyvevåbnet, the Royal Danish Air Force. Six of the aircraft are retained in the US for training purposes.

JSF founder member, later joined by Italy, the Netherlands, Denmark, Norway, Canada, Australia and Turkey.

### F-35A

The first F-35A flew in December 2006 but much publicized problems with many of its systems – the aircraft became briefly infamous because it 'couldn't fly in the rain' – coupled with initial performance shortfalls meant that it would be over 10 years before the F-35A achieved IOC (initial operating capability) with the USAF. By the beginning of 2025, the land-based F-35A had entered service with nine nations, with orders received from a further nine, and the aircraft had seen its first combat use, which took place in May 2018 in Israeli hands. By far the largest user is the US which intends to acquire a total of 2456 F-35s by 2044, of which 1763 will be F-35As, and operate the Lightning II until at least 2070.

FIGHTER AIRCRAFT

# Lockheed Martin F-35B/C Lightning II

> The F-35B and C are respectively STOVL (Short Take-Off and Vertical Landing) and carrier-capable variants of the Lightning II, both more complicated than the relatively conventional F-35A.

One of the aircraft that the F-35 was intended to replace was the Harrier in both US Marine Corps (USMC) and British service, and the F-35B sought to replicate that aircraft's unique vertical take-off and landing capability. Approximately a third of the aircraft's fuel load is sacrificed to accommodate a large fan, driven by a shaft from the Pratt & Whitney F135 engine that also features a thrust vectoring jet

This F-35B was pictured flying over the Atlantic during testing and carries inert AIM-9X Sidewinder missiles.

### Lockheed Martin F-35B

**Weight (maximum take-off):** 27,200kg (60,000lb)
**Dimensions:** Length 5.6m (51ft 3in), Wingspan 10.7m (35ft 0in), Height 4.36m (14ft 4in)
**Powerplant:** One Pratt & Whitney F135-PW-600 afterburning turbofan with shaft driven lift fan, rated at 120kN (27,000lbf) dry, 182kN (41,000lbf) in afterburner and 181kN (40,650lbf) hovering
**Maximum speed:** 2200km (1367 miles)
**Range:** 935km (505 miles) on internal fuel
**Ceiling:** 15,000m (50,000ft)
**Crew:** 1
**Armament:** One 25mm (0.98in) rotary cannon; up to 6,800kg (15,000lb) ordnance

## FIGHTER AIRCRAFT

**Opposite:**
This USMC F-35B Lightning II serves with VMFA 2111.

**Above & right:**
The front view of this F-35B shows the lift-fan door open. The Rolls-Royce lift fan is a 50-inch, two-stage contra-rotating fan capable of generating more than 20,000lbf of thrust.

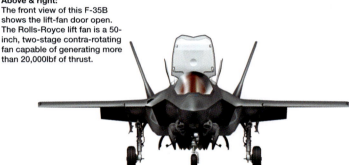

exhaust allowing for hovering flight. Although capable of taking off vertically when unloaded, the F-35B is considered a short take-off aircraft for operations, requiring a 'ski jump' ramp on aircraft carriers to take off with a combat payload, although it lands vertically. The F-35B has entered service with the USMC and Italian and Japanese Navies, and equips both the Royal Air Force and Royal Navy in the UK.

## F-35C

The F-35C was developed to fulfil the needs of the US Navy and replace the F/A-18 on US carriers. As a result it is intended for catapult launch and to make arrested landings aboard the USN's nuclear carrier fleet. The aircraft is easily distinguishable from the F-35A and B by its greater wingspan, and it also features folding wings to minimize its footprint at sea.

FIGHTER AIRCRAFT

# McDonnell Douglas F-4 Phantom II

> The West's most prolific supersonic aircraft, the Phantom has remained in constant service since 1960. Though nearing the end of its career, the F-4 still serves in numbers with three nations.

The prototype Phantom flew for the first time in 1958. Originally intended as a fleet defence fighter for the US Navy, the F4H Phantom was subsequently adopted by the US Air Force (USAF) as well who briefly designated it the F-110 Spectre before the F-4 designation was adopted universally. The type was flown by the Navy, Air Force and Marine Corps during the Vietnam War where

The final USAF role for the Phantom was as the QF-4 aerial target. Several of these aircraft were painted in heritage schemes such as the Vietnam war era colours seen here.

### McDonnell Douglas F-4E Phantom II

**Weight (maximum take-off):** 28,030kg (61,795lb)
**Dimensions:** Length 63ft 0in (19.2m), Wingspan 38ft 5in (11.7m), Height 6ft 5in (5m)
**Powerplant:** Two General Electric J79-GE-17A afterburning turbojet engines, each rated at 11,905lbf (52.96kN) thrust dry, 17,845lbf (79.38kN) with afterburner

**Maximum speed:** 2370km/h (1470mph)
**Range:** 3701km (2300 miles) ferry range
**Ceiling:** 60,000ft (18,000m)
**Crew:** 2
**Armament:** One 20mm (0.79in) M61A1 Vulcan cannon; up to 18,480kg (18,650lb) of ordnance and fuel on nine hardpoints

FIGHTER AIRCRAFT

**Opposite top:**
Japan flew the Phantom II for 50 years, retiring the last of its locally manufactured F-4EJ-KAIs, as pictured, in 2021.

**Above & below:**
Turkey concluded that there was still a place for the F-4 in its 21st-century inventory and upgraded its F-4E fleet in 2000 with Israeli avionics and systems, designating the improved aircraft the Terminator 2020.

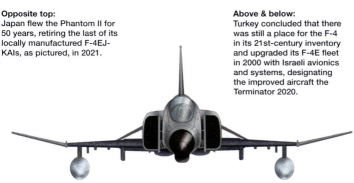

it built up an enviable reputation. All five US personnel who became 'aces' during the conflict with five or more victories were F-4 crew, but this came at a considerable cost: 678 Phantoms were lost, the majority to surface-to-air missiles (SAMs).

### Seven decades of service

Although the F-4 left US service in 1996, in 2025 the type was exported to 12 other nations and continues in service in Greece, Iran and Turkey. Greece is due to retire its F-4s soon but the 54 aircraft comprising Turkey's upgraded F-4E Terminator 2020 fleet are expected to remain operational until at least 2030. The status of the Iranian F-4s is less clear though 62 examples were reportedly on strength as late as 2021, despite a US embargo on the supply of spare parts since 1979.

FIGHTER AIRCRAFT

# McDonnell Douglas F/A-18 Hornet

**Although the Northrop YF-17 lost to the F-16 in the US Air Force's 'Lightweight Fighter Program', the aircraft was further developed into the F/A-18 to become the US Navy's primary combat type.**

Charged with acquiring a cheaper fighter than the F-14, the US Navy evaluated the two Lightweight Fighter Program entries in the 1970s and rejected the winning F-16 due to its narrow undercarriage and single-engine design, instead asking McDonnell Douglas to partner with Northrop to develop the aircraft into the carrier-capable F-18. The addition of the ability to deliver ground

A Canadian F-18 Hornet from the 409th Tactical Fighter Squadron launches a laser-guided bomb during evaluation.

## McDonnell Douglas F/A-18

**Weight (maximum take-off):** 21,888kg (48,253lb)
**Dimensions:** Length 17.07m (56ft 0in), Wingspan 11.43m (37ft 6in), Height 4.66m (15ft 4in)
**Powerplant:** Two General Electric F404-GE-402 afterburning turbofan engines, each rated at 11,000lbf (49kN) thrust, 17,750lbf (79.0kN) with afterburner

**Maximum speed:** 1915km/h (1190mph)
**Range:** 2017km (1253 miles)
**Ceiling:** 15,000m (50,000ft)
**Crew:** 1
**Armament:** 20mm (0.787in) M61A1 Vulcan 6-barrel rotary cannon; up to 6,200kg (13,700lb) ordnance and fuel on nine hardpoints

# FIGHTER AIRCRAFT

**Below (both images):**
The F/A-18D replaced the A-6 Intruder in the precision attack role and the job of the Hornet's second crew member is to operate the sophisticated avionics/sensor suite. This Marine Corps F/A-18D of VMFA(AW)-225 is armed with 127mm (5in) Zuni unguided rockets underwing, used for target-marking in the forward air controller role.

**Opposite:**
Canada has operated the CF-18 as a land-based interceptor since 1982. An unusual feature of CF-18s is the false canopy painted under the fuselage nose to confuse enemy aircrew.

attack stores and function in both the fighter and attack roles saw the aircraft reclassified as the F/A-18. Appearing in 1978, the aircraft entered US service with the US Marine Corps (USMC) in 1983 and with the Navy in 1984. After the appearance of the much improved, and larger, Super Hornet, the 'Legacy Hornet' was withdrawn from carrier operations. The Hornet remains in service with the US Marine Corps in 2025.

## Legacy Hornets

Although never eliciting the levels of export success as the F-16, the F/A-18 nevertheless attracted the attention of a number of nations around the world. Though Australia has now retired the Hornet, Canada, Finland, Kuwait, Malaysia, Spain and Switzerland all retain legacy Hornets in their inventories.

FIGHTER AIRCRAFT

# McDonnell Douglas/Boeing F/A-18 Super Hornet

> A considerably enlarged aircraft compared to earlier Hornet models, the Super Hornet comprises over 90% of the US Navy's carrier-capable combat aircraft fleet.

Appearing in single- and twin-seat form as the F/A-18E and F/A-18F respectively, the Super Hornet retained only the general layout and designation of the earlier Hornet and was in most respects an entirely new design. Intended primarily as a comparatively low-cost stop-gap while projects for a new 'Advanced Attack' (A-X) and 'Navy Advanced Tactical Fighter' (NATF) aircraft were developed, both these

Photographed in February 2025, these US Navy Super Hornets are assigned to the *Harry S Truman* Carrier Strike Group.

## Boeing F/A-18E Super Hornet

**Weight (maximum take-off):** 29,937kg (66,000lb)
**Dimensions:** Length 18.31m (60ft 1in), Wingspan 13.62m (44ft 8.5in), Height 4.88m (16ft)
**Powerplant:** Two General Electric F414-GE-400 turbofans, each rated at 58kN (13,000lbf) thrust dry, 98kN (22,000lbf) with afterburner

**Maximum speed:** 1915km/h (1190mph)
**Range:** 3330km (2070 miles) ferry range with maximum fuel
**Ceiling:** 15,940m (52,300ft)
**Crew:** 1
**Armament:** 20mm (0.787in) M61A1 Vulcan 6-barrel rotary cannon; up to 8,050kg (17,750lb) ordnance and fuel on 11 hardpoints

FIGHTER AIRCRAFT

**Above:**
As the US Navy's west coast F/A-18 Fleet Replacement Squadron, VFA-122 undertakes the training of Navy and Marine Corps Super Hornet Replacement Pilots and Weapon Systems Officers.

**Opposite top:**
VFA-14 'The Top Hatters' is the oldest active US Naval squadron, having formed in 1919. The squadron converted from the F-14 to the F/A-18E in 2002 and has operated the type ever since.

**Above:**
The Royal Australian Air Force selected the two-seat Super Hornet to replace the F-111, acquiring 24 F/A-18Fs in 2009.

programmes were abandoned and the Super Hornet subsequently became the only combat type on US carriers between 2006 and 2019.

### Navy flyer
Flown for the first time in late 1995, the aircraft entered fleet service in 1999. Since then it has played an important role in all active operations in which the US Navy has taken part.

Despite its ubiquity in the US Navy, the Super Hornet has not proved as successful as its predecessor on the export market, despite Boeing promoting the aircraft to a large number of potential operators, particularly those equipped with the Legacy Hornet, the type being touted as a logical progression from the earlier aircraft. Despite these efforts, only Australia and Kuwait have elected to acquire the type.

FIGHTER AIRCRAFT

# McDonnell Douglas/Boeing EA-18 Growler

A specialized Super Hornet derivative, the Growler is optimized for the electronic warfare mission, primarily as a jamming platform but also with combat capability.

Intended as a replacement for the ageing four-seat EA-6 Prowler, the Growler utilizes the same ALQ-99 jamming pod as the Prowler, but advances in digital technology and automation mean that a crew of two can now achieve better results than were achievable with the EA-6's crew of four. Since then the EA-18 fleet has received more advanced offensive jamming equipment such as the AN/

An EA-18G Growler of (VAQ) 129 lands on the flight deck of the aircraft carrier USS *George Washington*.

### Boeing EA-18G Growler

**Weight (maximum take-off):** 29,964kg (66,000lb)
**Dimensions:** Length 18.31m (60ft 1in), Wingspan 13.62m (44ft 9in), Height 4.88m (16ft)
**Powerplant:** Two General Electric F414-GE-400 turbofans, each rated at 58kN (13,000lbf) thrust dry, 98kN (22,000lbf) with afterburner

**Maximum speed:** 1900km/h (1190mph)
**Range:** 2346km (1458 miles)
**Ceiling:** 15,940m (52,300ft)
**Crew:** 2
**Armament:** Up to 8050kg (17,750lb) of ordnance and fuel on nine hardpoints

FIGHTER AIRCRAFT

**Above:**
VAQ-129 is permanently stationed at Naval Air Station Whidbey Island, in Puget Sound, Washington, and undertakes the training of all EA-18 aircrew.

**Opposite top:**
'Shadowhawks' is the nickname of US Navy Electromagnetic Attack Squadron 141 (VAQ-141). In 2011, this unit conducted the Growler's first combat missions of the EA-18G at sea in support of US operations over Iraq.

**Above:**
This EA-18 is operated by VAQ-134 which has flown the Growler since 2016.

ALQ-249 'Next Generation Jammer' that utilizes Active Electronically Scanned Arrays (AESA) and which achieved initial operating capability in 2021.

## Multirole fighter

The Growler also retains the excellent performance of its Super Hornet forebear and although primarily utilized to intercept, process and jam received radio frequency signals, the aircraft has the ability to carry an offensive armament as well as AIM-120 AMRAAM air-to-air missiles for self defence. In active US Navy service since 2009, the Growler scored its first air-to-air victory in 2024 when an EA-18 destroyed a Houthi drone during operations in the Red Sea.

The EA-18 has also been adopted by Australia with 12 examples ordered for the Royal Australian Air Force to complement its Super Hornet fleet.

FIGHTER AIRCRAFT

# McDonnell Douglas AV-8B Harrier II

> For many years the world's only vertical take-off and landing (VTOL) fixed-wing combat aircraft, the Harrier occupied a unique niche in military aviation and continues to serve with three nations.

Derived from the British-designed Harrier, which was operated by the US Marine Corps (USMC) as the AV-8A until 1987, the AV-8B was developed by McDonnell Douglas primarily with the aim of improving the Harrier's load-carrying ability and range. First flown in November 1978, the AV-8B entered US service in 1985 and was also adopted by the Navies of Italy and Spain, and all three

A USMC AV-8B Harrier II aircraft prepares to land aboard the amphibious assault ship USS *Peleliu* in September 2014.

## AV-8B Harrier II Plus

**Weight (maximum take-off):** 14,100kg (31,000lb)
**Dimensions:** Length 14.12m (46ft 4in), Wingspan 9.25m (30ft 4in), Height 3.55m (11ft 8in)
**Powerplant:** One Rolls-Royce Pegasus F402-RR-408 (Mk 107) vectored-thrust turbofan, rated at 105kN (23,500lbf) thrust

**Maximum speed:** 1083km/h (673mph)
**Range:** 2200km (1400 miles)
**Ceiling:** 15,240m (50,000ft)
**Crew:** 1
**Armament:** One General Dynamics GAU-12 Equalizer 25mm (0.98in) 5-barreled rotary cannon; up to 4200kg (9200lb) of fuel and ordnance

FIGHTER AIRCRAFT

**All images:**
This AV-8B Night Attack jet was serving with USMC VMA-214 'Black Sheep' in 1989. The unit made its first foreign deployment with the Harrier to Iwakuni, Japan, in October of that year. The aircraft carries a mixed load of two AGM-65E Mavericks, a pair of Mk 20 Rockeye cluster bombs and AIM-9L/M Sidewinders for self-defence.

nations continue to operate the aircraft in 2025. A British-built variant featuring a different wing was operated as the BAe Harrier II from 1989 until the fleet's somewhat controversial retirement in 2011.

### Combat role

Harrier IIs have seen considerable active service since their introduction, first used in combat in 1991 during the first Gulf War. Subsequently, AV-8Bs from all three nations to operate the type flew operations over the former Yugoslavia in the late 1990s and USMC Harriers have undertaken close support duties in Iraq and Afghanistan. The aircraft is due to be replaced by the F-35B in US service during 2026.

FIGHTER AIRCRAFT

# McDonnell Douglas F-15A–C Eagle

> Despite making its maiden flight over 50 years ago, the F-15 remains one of the world's finest air superiority fighters and boasts an unrivalled combat record.

When the Mcdonnell Douglas F-15 prototype first flew in July 1972, even the most sanguine of observers could scarcely have imagined that in 2025 the Eagle would still be in frontline service and would officially be credited with over 100 aircraft shot down (the majority with the Israeli Air Force) yet suffered not a single loss in aerial combat. The F-15A, which entered service in 1976, has now disappeared

An F-15C Eagle takes off during Weapons School Integration 21-B at Nellis Air Force Base, Nevada, 2021.

## McDonnell Douglas F-15C

**Weight (maximum take-off):** 30,844kg (68,000lb)
**Dimensions:** Length 19.43m (63ft 9in), Wingspan 13.06m (42ft 10in), Height 5.64m (18ft 6in)
**Powerplant:** Two Pratt & Whitney F100-PW-220 afterburning turbofans, each rated at 64.9kN (14,590lbf) thrust dry, 105.7kN (23,770lbf) with afterburner
**Maximum speed:** 2602km/h (1617mph)
**Range:** 4217km (2620 miles), with drop tanks
**Ceiling:** 20,000m (65,000ft)
**Crew:** 1
**Armament:** One 20mm (0.787in) M61A1 Vulcan 6-barrel rotary cannon; up to 7,300kg (16,000lb) ordnance and fuel

FIGHTER AIRCRAFT

**All images:**
This F-15C Eagle wears the markings of the 58th Tactical Fighter Squadron of the 33rd Fighter Wing. This aircraft accounted for four of the 58th TFS's 16 'kills' in the 1991 Gulf War. It is armed with AIM-7 Sparrow medium range air-to-air missiles on the fuselage pylons and AIM-9 Sidewinders under the wings in addition to carrying a large fuel load.

from US service, the last being withdrawn in 2009, but continues to serve with Israel. However, an improved single-seater, the F-15C, of which 483 were built between 1979 and 1985, remains in service with the US Air Force. The F-15C also serves as the basis for Japan's F-15J, over 150 of which were built under licence by Mitsubishi, making Japan the largest F-15 user outside America. Saudi Arabia also operates single-seat F-15Cs in the air superiority role.

**Extended service**
It was intended that the F-15C would be replaced during the 2010s by the F-22 Raptor, but the severely curtailed production run of the later aircraft due to its immense cost has seen the F-15C's retirement pushed back and a series of upgrades performed to keep the aircraft viable, adding improved AESA radar, improved avionics and infrared search and track (IRST) pods.

FIGHTER AIRCRAFT

# McDonnell Douglas F-15E 'Strike Eagle'

> The F-15E saw the air superiority single-seater evolve into a two-seat strike fighter. Despite initial disinterest in official circles, the F-15E came to outnumber single-seat F-15s in the US Air Force.

McDonnell Douglas began development of a multirole two-seat F-15, derived from the F-15B training variant, as a private venture, envisioning the aircraft as a replacement for the F-111 and F-4 in the interdiction role while retaining the ability to function as an effective air superiority asset. The US Air Force (USAF) issued a requirement for an 'Enhanced Tactical Fighter' to replace

An F-15E Strike Eagle taxis at Balad Air Base, Iraq, after a mission in support of Operation Iraqi Freedom during 2009.

## McDonnell Douglas F-15E

**Weight (maximum take-off):** 36,741kg (81,000lb)
**Dimensions:** Length 19.45m (63ft 10in), Wingspan 13.05m (42ft 10in), Height 5.64m (18ft 6in)
**Powerplant:** Two Pratt & Whitney F100-PW-220 afterburning turbofan, each rated at 64.9kN (14,590lbf) thrust dry, 105.7kN (23,770lbf) with afterburner
**Maximum speed:** 2655km/h (1650mph)
**Range:** 3900km (2400 miles)
**Ceiling:** 18,000m (60,000ft)
**Crew:** 2
**Armament:** One 20mm (0.787in) M61A1 Vulcan 6-barrel rotary cannon; up to 10,400kg (23,000lb) ordnance and fuel

# FIGHTER AIRCRAFT

**Opposite:**
The LN tailcode reveals this Strike Eagle is based at RAF Lakenheath, UK. It is on the strength of the 492nd Fighter Squadron, the 'Madhatters'.

**Right & below:**
Another Lakenheath-based Strike Eagle, this aircraft was serving with the 48th Fighter Wing. It is shown here loaded with 14 unguided bombs, as well as Sidewinders for self-defence.

the F-111 in 1981 and the F-15E emerged the winner in 1984, beating the rival F-16XL. The USAF received 236 examples between 1988 and 2001, gaining the useful but initially unofficial nickname of 'Strike Eagle' in US service.

## Superb strike aircraft

Despite being derived from an aircraft specifically designed for the air superiority mission, the F-15E has proven an extremely capable strike aircraft, serving with considerable success in Operation Desert Storm and subsequent US military operations ever since with over 200 F-15Es remaining in active service by 2025. The obvious capability and versatility offered by the F-15E has seen it enjoy some success on the export market, with the F-15I Ra'am ('Thunder') operated by Israel, the F-15K in South Korea, the F-15S of Saudi Arabia and the F-15SG flown by Singapore.

FIGHTER AIRCRAFT

# McDonnell Douglas/Boeing F-15EX Eagle II

> The latest iteration of the F-15 utilizes the two-seat platform of the F-15E and incorporates a selection of upgrades to maintain the Eagle's capability well into the 21st century.

A serious shortfall in US Air Force (USAF) fighter numbers in the 2010s was brought about by the much reduced F-22 order, caused by budgetary constraints coupled with serious delays to the F-35 programme and a rapidly ageing F-15 fleet. Consideration was given to reopening the F-22 production line, but for economic reasons it was decided to procure F-15s featuring all

Above & opposite: An F-15EX Eagle II of the 142nd Wing taxies and takes off during the official unveiling ceremony for the new fighter jet at the Portland Air National Guard Base in July 2024.

### Boeing F-15EX

**Weight (maximum take-off):** 36,741kg (81,000lb)
**Dimensions:** Length 19.45m (63ft 10in), Wingspan 13.05m (42ft 10in), Height 5.64m (18ft 6in)
**Powerplant:** Two General Electric F110-GE-129 afterburning turbofans, each rated at 76.31kN (17,155lbf) dry, 131kN (29,500lbf) with afterburner
**Maximum speed:** 2655km/h (1650mph)
**Range:** 3900km (2400 miles) with external fuel
**Ceiling:** 20,000m (65,000ft)
**Crew:** 2
**Armament:** One 20mm (0.787in) M61A1 Vulcan 6-barrel rotary cannon; up to 13,400kg (29,500lb) ordnance and fuel

FIGHTER AIRCRAFT

**Opposite:**
This aircraft, serialled 20-001, is the first production F-15EX to be built and is shown here in the colours of the 96th Test Wing based at Eglin Air Force Base.

**Below:**
Saudi Arabia has operated the F-15E since the 1990s and it was the substantial update of their fleet to F-15SA standard that served as the basis for the USAF F-15EX.

the upgrades incorporated onto the export F-15 'Advanced Eagle' operated by Saudi Arabia and Qatar for USAF use.

### Variants

Single-seat (F-15CX) and two-seat (F-15EX) variants were proposed but it was decided to obtain solely two-seaters as only the two-seat F-15 production line was in operation and this would minimize delays and production costs. The F-15EX, although not as survivable as the stealthy F-22 and F-35, remains an extremely potent combat aircraft primarily intended to replace the F-15C and complement the F-22 in the air superiority role. It can also operate as an effective ground attack aircraft in the mould of the F-15E. First flown in 2021, eight F-15EXs had been delivered by 2025 of a planned fleet of 104.

FIGHTER AIRCRAFT

# Mikoyan Gurevich MiG-21 'Fishbed'

One of the most important fighters in history, and the world's most produced supersonic aircraft, the elderly MiG-21 still serves in some numbers with several air forces.

First appearing in production form in 1959, having first flown four years earlier, the MiG-21 was originally a lightweight interceptor but was incrementally modified over decades to become a useful multirole type. Agile and possessing excellent performance, yet cheap enough to be acquired by developing nations, the MiG-21 found ready acceptance on the world market and was for several

Finland was the first non-Warsaw Pact nation to purchase the MiG-21 and operated the type from 1963 to 1998.

### MiG-21SM

**Weight (maximum take-off):** 9400kg (20,723lb)
**Dimensions:** Length 14.9m (48ft 11in), Wingspan 7.15m (23ft 6in), Height 4.71m (15ft 5in)
**Powerplant:** One Tumansky R-13F-300 afterburning turbojet engine rated at 39.9kN (8970lbf) dry, 63.7kN (14320lbf) with afterburner

**Maximum speed:** 2230km/h (1386mph)
**Range:** 1420km (882 miles)
**Ceiling:** 18,000m (59,055ft)
**Crew:** 1
**Armament:** One 23mm Gryazev-Shipunov GSh-23L cannon fixed, forward firing in ventral fairing; up to 1300kg (2866lb) bombs, missiles or stores

# FIGHTER AIRCRAFT

**Opposite:**
India is replacing the MiG-21 with the HAL Tejas, ending over 60 years of service with the Indian Air Force. This MiG-21PF serving in late 1971 featured irregular unit-level applied camouflage.

**Both images:**
The Syrian Air Force retained the MiG-21 in its inventory in 2025 though the future of the fleet is uncertain following the overthrow of the Assad regime. Early model aircraft such as this MiG-21F-13 suffered appalling losses during the Six-Day War and Yom Kippur War with Israel.

years the most widely used fighter in the world. Its appearance in Warsaw Pact air forces was hardly surprising but the qualities of the MiG were of sufficient merit to see it incorporated into the inventories of several non-aligned nations such as India and Finland. The former nation was so taken with it that it was produced under licence by Hindustan Aeronautics in Nasik and India was still operating two squadrons of MiG-21s as late as 2025.

## Veteran service

Although by 2025 it had largely disappeared from the inventories of the 60 or so nations that had operated the type from the 1960s onwards, significant numbers of the MiG-21 continue to serve with Angola, Cuba, North Korea and Syria.

FIGHTER AIRCRAFT

# Mikoyan Gurevich MiG-23 'Flogger'

> Developed as a replacement for the MiG-21, the MiG-23 was intended to offer improved performance, range and take-off performance while carrying more capable avionics and weapons.

Over 5000 MiG-23s were built over its production life, making this the most produced swing wing aircraft in history, and by 1990 around 1500 examples of this aircraft were in service with the Soviet Air Force. Unlike the MiG-21, the MiG-23 was equipped to fire beyond-visual-range (BVR) missiles, rendering it an order of magnitude more formidable than the earlier fighter. Although the type

The MiG-23 serves in small numbers with both factions vying for power in post-Gaddafi Libya. This one was being displayed in Tripoli in 2015.

## MiG-23MLD

**Weight (maximum take-off):** 17,800kg (39,242lb)
**Dimensions:** Length 16.7m (54ft 9in) Wingspan 13.97m (45ft 10in) wings spread, 7.78m (25ft 10in) wings fully swept
**Powerplant:** One Khatchaturov R-35-300 turbojet engine, rated at 83.6kN (18,800lbf) dry, 127.49kN (28660lbf) with afterburner

**Maximum speed:** 2500km/h (1600mph)
**Range:** 1450km (900 miles)
**Ceiling:** 18,500m (60,700ft)
**Crew:** 1
**Armament:** One 23mm (0.91in) Gryazev-Shipunov GSh-23L twin-barrelled Gast cannon fixed forward firing in lower forward fuselage

FIGHTER AIRCRAFT

**Opposite:**
India operated both the MiG-23 and MiG-27 and built 165 MiG-23Ms under licence. This example is a ground attack MiG-23BN with its distinctive radarless nose.

**Both images:**
Cuba is one of the last MiG-23 operators, with around 24 believed to remain in service. The MiG-23 fleet is finished in this distinctive camouflage scheme. The swept-wing mechanism is obvious from the front angle (shown right).

garnered an unfortunate reputation for accidents in its early career, particularly with regard to its engine which was prone to catastrophic failure, later examples were much improved and far more reliable, as well as featuring much improved manoeuvrability, allowing them to be flown as true air superiority fighters. A separate line of aircraft optimized for the fighter bomber role was developed as the MiG-23B which later evolved into the dedicated ground attack MiG-27 variant, though this has now been retired worldwide.

## Service today

Today the MiG-23 continues to serve in reasonable numbers in the air forces of Angola, Ethiopia, North Korea and Syria, though Israel has claimed the destruction of around 40 Syrian MiG-23s during ground operations in 2024.

FIGHTER AIRCRAFT

# Mikoyan Gurevich MiG-29 'Fulcrum'

The supremely agile MiG-29 remains in service with over 20 nations, most of which have been subject to upgrades. Russia retains around 150 single-seaters and 30 two-seaters on strength.

During the early 1970s the Soviet Union developed a 'light' fighter project to complement the 'heavy' Su-27 and intended primarily to function as an air superiority fighter. The programme mirrored the development of the 'heavy' F-15 and comparatively lightweight F-16 in the US and resulted in the appearance of the highly successful MiG-29. First flight of the MiG-29 took place on 6 October

A Polish Air Force MiG-29 taxis in with parachute in tow after finishing a mission at Poznan Air Base.

## Mikoyan Gurevich MiG-29S

**Weight (maximum take-off):** 19,700kg (42,680lb)
**Dimensions:** Length 17.32m (56ft 10in), Wingspan 11.36m (37ft 3in), Height 4.73m (15ft 6in)
**Powerplant:** Two Klimov RD-33 afterburning turbofan engines each rated at 49.42kN (11110lbf) dry and 81.39kN (18298lbf)

**Maximum speed:** 2445km/h (1519mph)
**Range (without external tanks):** 1500km (932 miles)
**Ceiling:** 17,000m (55,775ft)
**Crew:** 1
**Armament:** One 30mm (1.18in) Gryazev-Shipunov GSh-30-1 cannon; up to 4000kg (8818lb) of bombs, missiles or stores

# FIGHTER AIRCRAFT

**Above:**
Yugoslavia received 14 MiG-29Bs and 2 MiG-29UBs from the Soviet Union in 1987 and 1988. Several were shot down by NATO aircraft during the conflict in the Balkans and the five surviving aircraft are now operated by Serbia.

**Opposite top:**
Belarus maintains a force of 32 MiG-29s, 13 of which were upgraded to MiG-29BM standard in 2004.

**Above:**
'07 Blue' was one of five MiG-29s that displayed at Zhukovsky in 2012 during celebrations to mark the centenary of the Russian Air Force. Russia retains around 200 MiG-29s in its inventory.

1977 and, after 14 development aircraft were built, the first pre-series aircraft flew in early 1979, followed by production aircraft in the summer of 1982.

## Export sales

The MiG-29 was officially commissioned into service in 1987, after various improvements had been made, but had actually first become operational during 1980, with a detachment of aircraft being based at Wittstock, East Germany, in 1986. Export sales have been strong, with around 40 nations acquiring examples of the Fulcrum. The largest non-Russian user is India, with a fleet of around 65 MiG-29s in service, all of which were significantly upgraded in 2016. Meanwhile, most Russian examples are now of the MiG-29SMT variant with many internal improvements and greater fuel load carried in a much enlarged spine.

FIGHTER AIRCRAFT

# Mikoyan Gurevich MiG-29K 'Fulcrum'

The carrier-capable version of the Fulcrum, the MiG-29K is superficially similar to the original MiG-29 but uses an all-new airframe with a larger wing.

The project to develop a carrier-capable Fulcrum dates back to the 1980s, with plans to equip an air wing for the Soviet Navy's planned carrier fleet. The first MiG-29K prototype featuring double-slotted flaps, leading-edge vortex controllers, arrester hook and other naval features took to the air in June 1988 before making its first carrier landing on the carrier *Tbilisi* (later renamed *Admiral Kuznetsov*) on

A brand new unpainted MiG-29K of the Russian Navy performs a test flight at Zhukovsky.

### Mikoyan Gurevich MiG-29K

**Weight (maximum take-off):** 22,400kg (49,384lb)
**Dimensions:** Length 17.3m (56ft 9in), Wingspan 11.99m (39ft 4in), Height 4.4m (14ft 5in)
**Powerplant:** Two Klimov RD-33MK turbofan engines, each rated at 52.96kN (11,905llbf) thrust dry

**Maximum speed:** 2200km/h (1370mph)
**Range:** 1850km (1150 miles)
**Ceiling:** 17,500m (57,415ft)
**Crew:** 1
**Armament:** One 30mm (1.2in) Gryazev-Shipunov GSh-30-1 cannon in the port leading edge root extension; up to 4500kg (9920lb) of weapons and stores on nine hardpoints

# FIGHTER AIRCRAFT

**Above:**
Another aircraft of the 100th Independent Shipborne Fighter Aviation Regiment is '42 Blue', shown here with external tanks.

**Opposite top:**
'34 Blue' is a MiG-29K of the 100th Independent Shipborne Fighter Aviation Regiment based at Severomorsk-3 Air Base near Murmansk in the north of Russia for operations with the Northern Fleet.

**Above:**
'31 Blue' was on display at Kubinka Airshow in 2023. The MiG-29K's long canopy is used for both twin and single-seat versions.

1 November 1989. In 1992, after the collapse of the Soviet Union, the project was abandoned but when the Indian Navy took delivery of the former Russian Navy carrier *Admiral Gorshkov*, and renamed it *Vikramaditya*, work on the MiG-29K resumed for Indian Navy use.

## Indian Navy

The first fighters for India were flown in March 2008 and in September 2009 an Indian MiG-29K landed for the first time on the deck of a Russian Navy aircraft carrier. The MiG-29K subsequently entered service with India in 2009. In 2012 Russia ordered 20 MiG-29KRs and four MiG-29KUBRs to serve aboard the sole Russian Navy aircraft carrier, *Admiral Kuznetsov*, the first example of which flew in October 2013.

FIGHTER AIRCRAFT

# Mikoyan Gurevich MiG-29M and MiG-35 'Fulcrum'

Developed in parallel with the carrier-capable MiG-29K, the MiG-29M and MiG-35 are land-based fighters utilizing the same airframe and avionics as the naval aircraft.

The MiG-29M and MiG-35 are essentially the same aircraft, with different designations depending on marketing. Development of an advanced, multirole version of the MiG-29 originally began in the 1980s and six MiG-29Ms were completed before the USSR collapsed, the first flying in April 1986. Like the related MiG-29K, the project was abandoned in the aftermath of the end of the

A MiG-35 displays at the MAKS 2015 air show at Zhukovsky air base near Moscow.

### MiG-29M

**Weight (maximum take-off):** 24,500kg (54,013lb)
**Dimensions:** Length 17.3m (56ft 9in), Wingspan 11.99m (39ft 4in), Height 4.4m (14ft 5in)
**Powerplant:** Two Klimov RD-33MK turbofan engines, each rated at 52.96kN (11,905llbf) thrust dry and 88.3kN (19,840lbf) with afterburning

**Maximum speed:** 2100km/h (1300mph)
**Range:** 2000km (1240 miles)
**Ceiling:** 16,000m (52,493ft)
**Crew:** 1 or 2
**Armament:** One 30mm (1.2in) Gryazev-Shipunov GSh-30-1 cannon in the port leading edge root extension; up to 6500kg (14,330lb) of weapons and stores on nine hardpoints

## FIGHTER AIRCRAFT

**Opposite:**
'702 Blue' is a pre-production single-seater MiG-35 shown here as it appeared during tests with Russian Aerospace Forces in January 2017.

**Right (both images):**
One of the first six MiG-29Ms built before the collapse of the Soviet Union, '156 Blue' was displayed at Farnborough Airshow in the UK in 1992. The project languished for nearly 20 years until the first new MiG-29M flew in 2011.

Soviet Union for a time but was revived over a decade later. Although closely related to the naval MiG-29K, the MiG-35 deletes the arrester hook and refuelling probe, does not feature wing folding and discards maritime navigation equipment.

### Syrian service

First taking to the sky in two-seat form in December 2011 with the single-seat variant flying the following year, the first order was placed by Syria but this was not initially completed due to the outbreak of the Syrian civil war and Egypt became the first export customer, taking delivery of 46 MiG-29Ms in 2015. Subsequently 12 MiG-29SMTs were delivered to Syria in 2020. Algeria also operates the type. Russia ordered 24 MiG-35s and the aircraft has reportedly seen action in Ukraine.

FIGHTER AIRCRAFT

# Mikoyan Gurevich MiG-31 'Foxhound'

A huge interceptor of sensational performance, the Mach 2.8-capable MiG-31 was developed from the infamous MiG-25 'Foxbat' that had alarmed Western observers in the early 1970s.

The aircraft that became the MiG-31 was initially developed as a relatively straightforward two-seat MiG-25 variant featuring multi-target capability and extended endurance. This was designated the MiG-25MP, and made its first flight in September 1975. Extensively redesigned and redesignated to become the MiG-31, the aircraft entered production in 1976 and was declared fully operational

The MiG-31 was considerably heavier than the MiG-25, necessitating the use of its distinctive tandem wheel main undercarriage.

## MiG-31M

**Weight (maximum take-off):** 46,200kg (101,854lb)
**Dimensions:** Length 22.62m (74ft 3in), Wingspan 13.46m (44ft 2in), Height 6.46m (21ft 2in)
**Powerplant:** Two Soloviev D-30F6 afterburning turbofan engines, each rated at 93kN (21000lbf) dry, 152kN (34000lbf) with afterburner

**Maximum speed:** 3000km/h (1865mph)
**Range (with external fuel):** 3000km (1865 miles)
**Ceiling:** 25,000m (82,000ft)
**Crew:** 2
**Armament:** One 23mm (0.91in) Gryazev-Shipunov GSh-6-23M rotary cannon; up to 9000kg (20,000lb) of stores and ordnance

## FIGHTER AIRCRAFT

**Opposite:**
A well-travelled Foxhound, '374 White' displayed in this colourful scheme at the Paris Air Show in 1991, appearing at Farnborough the following year.

**Right (both images):**
The first MiG-31 seen in the West, '057 Blue' was the seventh MiG-31M to be built and included the improved Zaslon-M radar system. This variant fell victim to the lack of funds following the collapse of the Soviet Union.

with the Soviet Air Force in 1983, featuring the Zaslon fire-control system, the world's first operational electronically scanned phased-array fighter radar. As designed, four MiG-31s were intended to be able to defend an area of airspace along a front of up to 900km (560 miles).

## Russian service

Russian Aerospace Forces operate 130 MiG-31s, and the Russian Navy's Northern Fleet also maintains one MiG-31 squadron. A further 130 or so aircraft are in storage, some being returned to service after refurbishment, and the aircraft is expected to remain in service until at least 2030. During the invasion of Ukraine, MiG-31s have reportedly shot down several Ukrainian aircraft, mainly by using the long-range R-37 air-to-air missile. By remaining at high speed and high altitude, MiG-31s have remained largely immune to interception.

FIGHTER AIRCRAFT

# Mitsubishi F-2

A Japanese-built multirole F-16 derivative, the Mitsubishi F-2 is a multirole fighter, intended to operate effectively as both an interceptor and in the anti-shipping role.

Japan required a replacement for its rapidly ageing F-1 ground attack and anti-shipping aircraft. Derived from the F-16, the F-2 is larger overall and features a wing of 25% greater area allowing for the carriage of four anti-ship missiles, four short-range air-to-air missiles and two to four medium-range air-to-air missiles while also allowing decent range capability. Lockheed Martin had already

Above & top: All JASDF Mitsubishi F-2s are finished in this attractive two-tone blue scheme. The single-seaters are designated F-2A.

## Mitsubishi F-2A

**Weight (maximum take-off):** 22,100kg (48,722lb)
**Dimensions:** Length 15.52m (50ft 11in), Wingspan 11.125m (36ft 6in) including wingtip pylons, Height 16ft (4.9m)
**Powerplant:** One General Electric F110-IHI-129 turbofan rated at 131kN (29,500lb) thrust with afterburning

**Maximum speed:** Mach 1.7, 2100km/h (1305mph)
**Range:** 833km (518 miles)
**Ceiling:** 18,000m (59,000ft)
**Crew:** 1
**Armament:** One 20mm (0.787in) JM61A1 six-barrel rotary cannon, plus up to 8085kg (17,824lb) of ordnance and stores

FIGHTER AIRCRAFT

**Below:**
Two-seat F-2Bs are mainly assigned to 21 Hikotai and mostly used for training at Matsushima. The F-2B production run encompassed two XF-2B prototypes and 32 production examples.

**Right: The F-2's wing, as displayed by this F-2A in 2017, is larger than the F-16 and features a less acute sweep on the leading edge and forward sweep on the trailing edge, where the F-16 has none.**

undertaken design work on an enlarged F-16, named Agile Falcon, as a low-cost entry to the ATF contest (which was ultimately won by the F-22 Raptor).

## Japanese service

The F-2 utilizes the wing design of this unbuilt derivative and includes many other changes, most significantly Japanese avionics, a strengthened nose and three-section canopy. Performance of the new aircraft, which flew for the first time in October 1995, proved excellent but the F-2's astonishingly high cost, some four times that of a Block 50 F-16 of similar capability, proved controversial. Just under 100 production aircraft were delivered in total to the Japan Air Self-Defence Force (JASDF).

FIGHTER AIRCRAFT

# Northrop F-5

> Allthough quite an elderly airframe, the F-5 is still an important fighter asset for several air arms, notably those of Brazil, South Korea, Switzerland and Iran.

Developed as a lightweight low-cost fighter, specifically designed with longevity in mind, the F-5 first took to the air in July 1959 and served primarily with US allies in large numbers, notably in Canada, the Netherlands and South Vietnam. Most nations have now retired the aircraft but it serves on in Brazil, where its replacement by the Saab Gripen is intended to be complete by 2029,

The F-5 has performed as the 'enemy' in US combat training for many years. This aircraft is from the US Navy's VFC-111 'Sundowners', which still flies the F-5 as an aggressor.

## Northrop F-5E Tiger II

**Weight (maximum take-off):** 11,192kg (24,675lb)
**Dimensions:** Length 14.69m (48ft 2in), Wingspan 8.13m (26ft 8in), Height 4.08m (13ft 5in)
**Powerplant:** Two General Electric J85-GE-21 afterburning turbojet engines, rated at 16kN (3,500lbf) thrust each dry, 22kN (5,000lbf) with afterburner

**Maximum speed:** Mach 1.63, 1741km/h (1082mph)
**Range:** 891km (554 miles)
**Ceiling:** 15,800m (51,800ft)
**Crew:** 1
**Armament:** Two 20mm (0.79in) M39A2 Revolver cannon; up to 3200kg (7000lb) of ordnance and fuel on seven hardpoints

FIGHTER AIRCRAFT

**Opposite:**
The F-5 remains the most prolific fighter aircraft in the Brazilian inventory in the mid 2020s. The aircraft were updated to F-5EM standard with improved avionics and systems in the early 2000s.

**Both images:**
A Swiss Air Force Northrop F-5E Tiger II armed with AIM-9P Sidewinder infrared-guided missiles. Switzerland has operated the type since 1978 and intends to replace it with the F-35 in 2027.

as well as with South Korea, Switzerland and around a dozen other air forces, notably Iran.

## Iranian derivatives

The F-5 has proved sufficiently successful in Iran that three specific Iranian derivatives have appeared: the HESA Azarakhsh, which appears to be no more than a standard F-5E, the two-seat HESA Kowsar, which is reportedly fitted with updated avionics, and the HESA Saeqeh which features twin vertical tails and was first flown in 2004. Whether these aircraft are reverse-engineered new-build airframes or merely modifications of existing F-5s is not definitively known outside of Iran itself.

FIGHTER AIRCRAFT

# Saab JAS 39 Gripen

> The Gripen survived a problematic development to emerge as a highly effective and remarkably affordable lightweight supersonic multirole fighter and has been widely exported.

Combining the canard layout that Saab had utilized on its highly distinctive Viggen to a much lighter fighter utilizing fly-by-wire flight controls, the Gripen ('Griffin') initially courted controversy in Sweden due to the considerable cost of its development as well as a series of bribery scandals relating to the marketing of the aircraft. Two very well-publicized crashes leading to

A two-seat Gripen armed with Sidewinders and precision-guided munitions.

## Saab JAS 39C

**Weight (maximum take-off):** 14,000kg (30,865lb)
**Dimensions:** Length 14.9m (48ft 11in), Wingspan 8.4m (27ft 7in), Height 4.5m (14ft 9in)
**Powerplant:** One Volvo RM12 turbofan engine, rated at 54kN (12,000lbf) thrust dry, 80.5kN (18,100lbf) with afterburner

**Maximum speed:** Mach 2, 2100km/h (1300mph)
**Range:** 800km (500 miles)
**Ceiling:** 15,240m (50,000ft)
**Crew:** 1
**Armament:** One 27mm (1in) Mauser BK-27 revolver cannon; up to 5300kg (11,700lb) of ordnance and stores on eight hardpoints

FIGHTER AIRCRAFT

**Opposite:**
A Hungarian Air Force (Magyar Légiero) Gripen adorned with Tiger Meet artwork on the tail and external tank. Hungary operates 14 Gripens and ordered a further four in 2024.

**Right (both images):**
The first production JAS-39A Gripen for the Swedish Air Force (Svenska flygvapnet), shown armed with two RBS 15 anti-shipping missiles, two RB 75s (AGM-65 Mavericks) and two RB 74s (AIM-9 Sidewinders).

the loss of the first prototype and an early production aircraft in 1989 and 1993 respectively also undermined confidence in the type. Nonetheless, the Gripen is today regarded very favourably, having served in the Swedish Air Force since 1996. By 2025 a further five nations were operating the type, Brazil being the largest customer, and a single example is leased to the UK. Saab continues to market the type, with further sales expected.

## Low-cost flyer

Part of the Gripen's appeal is its low operating cost, delivering a cost per hour about a third lower than the closest fighter type, the F-16 Block 50. Despite its low cost the Gripen has demonstrated its excellence in air-to-air combat: on the first day of the Red Flag Alaska exercise of 2006, Gripens scored 10 'kills', including a Eurofighter Typhoon and five F-16 Block 50s, with no losses.

FIGHTER AIRCRAFT

# Shenyang J-8 'Finback'

Resembling a scaled-up MiG-21, the J-8 was subject to severe production delays and though the prototype flew in 1969, the J-8 only entered service in 1985.

Today, a development period lasting longer than a decade is far from unusual but in 1985 this represented a glacial pace, especially given that the J-8 was far from a cutting-edge design even in the late 1960s. The delay had initially been caused by the upheaval of the cultural revolution but even once the political situation stabilized, progress was slow. Nonetheless, through a series of redesigns and

A Shenyang J-8 lands at the 24th Air Division base, Yangcun, southeast of Beijing, in July 2002.

### Shenyang J-8F

**Weight (maximum take-off):** 15,288kg (33,704lb)
**Dimensions:** Length 21.39m (70ft 2in), Wingspan 9.34m (30ft 8in), Height 5.41m (17ft 9in)
**Powerplant:** Two Guizhou WP-13B afterburning turbojet engines, 47.1kN (10,580lbf) thrust each dry, 68.6kN (15,430lbf) with afterburner

**Maximum speed:** Mach 1.8
**Range:** 1000km (620 miles) with drop tanks
**Ceiling:** 18,000m (59,000ft)
**Crew:** 1
**Armament:** One 23mm (0.9in) Type 23-III cannon; one centreline and six under-wing hardpoints with a capacity of three drop tanks; two PL-11 missiles SARH AAM

FIGHTER AIRCRAFT

**Opposite:**
This J-8F was spotted at Changchun Dafangshen Airport in October 2019. The J-8F is equipped with PL-11 medium-range semi-active radar homing air-to-air missiles.

**Above:**
The JZ-8F is a reconnaissance version of the J-8F that replaces the Type 23-III cannon with an internal camera.

**Right:** A Shenyang J-8 is exhibited during a PLAAF demonstration day, 2015.

upgrades the Finback matured into an acceptably capable interceptor and strike aircraft that remains in service in China (the type was never exported), though it is now in the twilight of its career.

## J-8A

Initial deliveries of the J-8I (also referred to as the J-8A) began in 1985 though production was cut short in 1987 due to the aircraft failing to meet the specification of the People's Liberation Army Air Force (PLAAF), and a thorough redesign that introduced lateral intakes and a large nose radome resulted in a much more satisfactory aircraft that was serial produced from 1992. The final variant, the J-8G, intended for the SEAD role, entered service in 2002.

FIGHTER AIRCRAFT

# Shenyang J-11 'Flanker-B+'

China's 'Flanker', the licence-built Su-27SK known as the J-11, was initially broadly the same as Russian-built aircraft but has subsequently been developed into a quite different aircraft.

The licence production deal was signed in 1995 and the first Chinese-assembled Su-27 made its maiden flight in December 1998. By 2002 production had switched to the improved J-11A which featured an improved radar system intended to deliver true multirole capability. By 2006, however, the J-11B was being built which saw the aircraft equipped entirely with Chinese-produced

This two-seat J-11B was photographed during its display at the PLAAF air show at Dafangshen airport in September 2015.

## Shenyang J-11B

**Weight (maximum take-off):** 33,000kg (72,753lb)
**Dimensions:** Length 21.9m (69ft 6in), Wingspan 14.7m (48ft 3in), Height 5.92m (19ft 5in)
**Powerplant:** Two Shenyang WS-10A 'Taihang' afterburning turbofans, each rated at 132kN (30,000lbf) thrust

**Maximum speed:** Mach 2.35, 2500km/h (1553mph)
**Range:** 3530km (2190 miles)
**Ceiling:** 19,000m (62,000ft)
**Crew:** 1
**Armament:** One 30mm (1.18in) Gryazev-Shipunov GSh-30-1 cannon; 10 hardpoints with provisions for PL-12 and PL-15 missiles

# FIGHTER AIRCRAFT

**Above:**
This J-11A was displayed in this special scheme during celebrations for the 60th anniversary of the PLAAF, held at Beijing Shahezhen Air Base in November 2009. It is believed to be from the 4th Regiment of the 2nd Air Division, based at Liuzhou.

**Opposite top:**
This J-11A wears red stripe markings on the IR seeker, tail stinger and wing tip rails and a double stripe behind the canopy, as special markings for the 70th China Victory Day parade in August 2015.

**Above:**
The J-11B includes more Chinese-produced features, such as the WS-10 engines and redesigned wing tip pylons. It is painted in the dark blue 'gunship' scheme with solid black radome.

equipment, most notably its WS-10 engines, replacing the Russian AL-31Fs of earlier variants and a fully indigenous radar, flight control system, avionics and targeting systems. The J-11B also features a much greater use of composite materials than its Russian predecessors, resulting in a considerable decrease in structural weight.

## J-11BS trainer

A two-seat combat trainer variant has been developed, designated the J-11BS, as well as a carrier-capable variant for the Navy, the J-11BH. The latter variant became briefly famous in August 2014 after an example intercepted a US Navy P-8 Poseidon over the South China Sea, shadowed the P-8 at an extremely short distance – reportedly there was just 6m (20ft) separation between the aircraft's wingtips – and then performed a barrel roll above the American aircraft.

FIGHTER AIRCRAFT

# Shenyang J-16

Continuing with Shenyang's unlicensed Flanker derivatives, the J-16 apparently stems from China's desire not to purchase further two-seat Su-30s from Russia.

To meet this end the J-16 was developed which marries the two-seat airframe of the J-11BS with Chinese WS-10 engines and a wide array of domestically produced avionics. The aircraft therefore makes a clean break from earlier Russian-produced Flankers and likely delivers China's most capable tactical combat aircraft, with the possible exception of the J-20, and many of the technologies

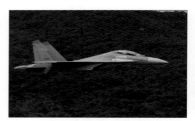

Shenyang J-16 at Airshow China in Zhuhai. The aircraft's Chinese name is 'Qianlong', which translates as 'Hidden Dragon'.

### Shenyang J-16

**Weight (maximum take-off):** 35,000kg (77,162lb)
**Dimensions:** Length 21.9m (69ft 6in), Wingspan 14.7m (48ft 3in), Height 6.36m (20ft 9in)
**Powerplant:** Two Shenyang WS-10B afterburning turbofans, 135kN (30,000lbf) with afterburner

**Maximum speed:** Mach 2
**Range:** 3530km (2190 miles, 1,910nm)
**Ceiling:** 19,000m (62,000ft)
**Crew:** 2
**Armament:** One 30mm (1.18in) Gryazev-Shipunov GSh-30-1 cannon; unknown total weight of ordnance and stores carried on 12 external hardpoints

FIGHTER AIRCRAFT

**Above:**
This uncoded J-16D, displayed at Zhuhai International Airshow in September 2021, carries the diagnostic ICM pods of the type and, on pylons beneath the wings and intake cheeks, are various jamming pods. A pair of missiles are carried in tandem on the belly centreline.

**Opposite top:**
Serving with the 3rd Brigade of the Northern Command, this J-16 carries a pair of rocket pods, mounted side-by-side on a single pylon, under its wings. Each pod contains five 122mm (4.8in) folding fin unguided rockets.

**Above:**
This J-16 is from the Eastern Command's 98th Air Brigade based at Chongqing and is armed with a PL-10 imaging infrared air-to-air missile on the wingtip and PL-15 radar guided air-to-air missile beneath its wings.

developed for that aircraft have been incorporated into the J-16. Little is definitely known about the development of the J-16 but it is believed to have flown for the first time in October 2011 and production began around two years later. By mid 2015 the type had entered air force service.

## Superior Flanker

Externally, the type resembles the Su-30MKK, also operated by the People's Liberation Army Air Force (PLAAF), but it features a greater use of composites in its structure, reducing weight, as well as a suite of more advanced avionics and longer-ranged weapons. As a result the J-16 is considered to be the most advanced and formidable of all Flanker variants so far constructed. Over 350 are reported to have been built by 2025 and production continues.

FIGHTER AIRCRAFT

# Shenyang J-31/J-35

> Still in the advanced stages of testing in 2025, the stealthy, supersonic, multirole J-31/J-35 will soon become the latest combat aircraft to enter People's Liberation Army Air Force (PLAAF) service.

Intended to supply an alternative to the F-35 at a comparatively affordable price for nations unable to join the F-35 programme, whether that be for political reasons or cost, and superficially resembling a twin-engined version of the American aircraft, the J-31 has been the subject of considerable speculation as to its capability and performance. The prototype was first displayed in

A Shenyang FC-31 performs during the China International Aviation & Aerospace Exhibition in Zhuhai, 2014.

### Shenyang FC-31 (prototype)

**Weight (maximum take-off):** 28,000kg (61,729lb)
**Dimensions:** 17.3m (56ft 9in), Wingspan 11.5m (37ft 9in), Height 4.8m (15ft 9in)
**Powerplant:** Two Guizhou WS-13E afterburning turbofans, each rated at 87.2–93.2kN (19,600–21,000lbf) with afterburner

**Maximum speed (estimated):** Mach 1.8
**Range (estimated):** 2000km (1200 miles) with drop tanks
**Ceiling (estimated):** 16,000m (52,000ft)
**Crew:** 1
**Armament:** Up to 2000kg (4400lb) of ordnance in weapons bay, and up to 6000kg (13000lb) of ordnance or fuel on six external hardpoints

FIGHTER AIRCRAFT

**Right: A Chinese Shenyang J-31 stealth fighter pictured in front of the KJ-2000 AWACS, KJ-200 AEW&C and Xian Y-20 transport aircraft (left to right) of the PLAAF at the China air show, 2020.**

**Opposite & right:** Little is definitively known about the J-31 and J-35 – even the designations are unconfirmed. This aircraft is depicted in a possible service scheme.

public at the Zhuhai air show in November 2014 after a first flight about two years earlier. The aircraft was known as the FC-31 Gyrfalcon and had been constructed by Shenyang as a private venture after the design lost to the J-20 in the J-XX competition for the development of a fifth-generation fighter.

## Naval fighter

Despite being developed without government support, the aircraft has subsequently attracted official Chinese interest, initially to be developed as a naval fighter designated the J-35, and a navalized prototype with folding wings, catapult and arrester gear flew in October 2021. Pakistan has expressed its intention to acquire the type and Egypt has entered into talks regarding a possible acquisition.

FIGHTER AIRCRAFT

# Sukhoi Su-27 'Flanker'

**The finest fighter developed in the Soviet Union, the large and formidable Su-27 remains an important component of the air forces of several nations around the world.**

For many years the Su-27 was the most important fighter in the Russian inventory, although its importance is now diminishing. A 'heavy' long-range air superiority fighter and escort fighter, the Su-27 programme was launched in 1969 in response to the development of the McDonnell Douglas F-15. The first prototype T-10-1 made its maiden flight in May 1977 and though the design was

This Ukrainian Flanker was displayed at the Royal International Air Tattoo at Fairford, UK, in July 2017.

### Sukhoi Su-27SKM 'Flanker-B'

**Weight (maximum take-off):** 28,300kg (62,391lb)
**Dimensions:** Length 21.94m (72ft) without probe, Wingspan 14.7m (48ft 3in), Height 5.93m (19ft 6in)
**Powerplant:** Two Saturn AL-31F turbofans, each rated at 122.58kN (27,558lb) thrust with afterburning

**Maximum speed:** Mach 2.15, 2655km/h (1650mph)
**Range:** 3680km (2285 miles)
**Ceiling:** 18,000m (65,055ft)
**Crew:** 1
**Armament:** One GSh-301 30mm (1.2in) cannon, plus up to 8000kg (17640lb) of external stores on 10 weapons pylons

FIGHTER AIRCRAFT

**Above:**
The same aircraft as in the photo opposite, 'Blue 58' wears the highly distinctive 'digital' camouflage applied to several Ukrainian Flankers.

**Opposite top:**
This Su-27 bears the 'Z' marking applied to the equipment of Russian forces operating in Ukraine, more usually seen on ground attack aircraft and helicopters.

**Above:**
The Su-27S was the initial production single-seater with an improved AL-31F engine. 'Blue 15' serves with the Ukrainian Air Force.

heavily revised in the late 1970s, it entered frontline service in 1985. The following year a unique stripped-down version, designated the P-42, successfully beat several time-to-height records set by the F-15 'Streak Eagle', some of which still stand. Despite its large size, the Su-27 is noted for its astonishing manoeuvrability, and the aircraft became famous for its aerobatic performances at air shows in the West during the *perestroika* period.

## First kill

After the collapse of the USSR, various successor states became operators of the type and the Su-27 was exported to China, Ethiopia, Indonesia and Vietnam. Ethiopian Su-27s scored the type's first air-to-air victories in 1999, shooting down two Eritrean MiG-29s. Russian Su-27s have seen combat in Abkhazia, South Ossetia and Syria, and since 2022 the aircarft has been utilized by both sides in the Russo-Ukrainian war.

FIGHTER AIRCRAFT

# Sukhoi Su-30 'Flanker'

> The two-seat Flanker was developed in the late 1980s to transform the air-superiority-focused Su-27 into a long-range strike fighter with true multirole capability.

The concept behind the Su-30 began with the two-seat Su-27UB Flanker-C combat trainer, which retained operational capability but possessed the same fire-control system and weapons of the single-seat Su-27. The original Su-30, first flown in 1989, added a tactical situation display in the rear cockpit and an inflight refuelling probe. Only five were built due to the dire economic situation in

An Indian Air Force Sukhoi Su-30 Flanker aircraft lands at Nellis Air Force Base, US, during the 'Red Flag' exercises held in 2008.

### Sukhoi Su-30MKI 'Flanker-H'

**Weight (maximum take-off):** 34,000kg (74,957lb)
**Dimensions:** Length 21.94m (71ft 11in), Wingspan 14.7m (48ft 2in), Height 6.4m (20ft 11in)
**Powerplant:** Two AL-31FP (izdeliye 96) thrust-vectoring turbofans, each providing 122.6kN (27,550lbf) thrust at maximum afterburning

**Maximum speed:** 2120km/h (1320mph)
**Range:** 3000km (1864 miles)
**Ceiling:** 17,300m (56,758ft)
**Crew:** 2
**Armament:** One 30mm (1.2in) Gryazev-Shipunov GSh-30-1 Gast autocannon; up to 8130kg (17,920lb) of weapons and stores

# FIGHTER AIRCRAFT

**Above:**
Pictured as it appeared in 2022, '16 Red' is an Su-30SM. SM stands for Serijnyi Modernizirovannyi ('Serial Modernized') and features much improved weapons, avionics and systems over earlier Su-30 models.

**Opposite top:**
China has operated the Su-30 since 2001. This Sukhoi Su-30MKK belonged to the 54th Brigade at Changsha Air Base in September 2020.

**Above:**
Russian Naval Forces also operate the Su-30SM, such as '48 Blue' depicted here. Deliveries are ongoing to the navy in 2025 for a planned inventory of 50 aircraft.

post-Soviet Russia and the Su-30 was developed into the export-orientated Su-30MK.

Two lines of development have subsequently been pursued, each named after its production location. The 'Irkutsk Su-30' line began with the Su-30MKI for India, developed and built in cooperation with Hindustan Aircraft Limited (HAL) and is the more advanced aircraft. These Flankers are characterized by their canard foreplanes, thrust-vectoring engines and an open-architecture fire-control system based around the electronically scanned Bars radar.

## Chinese Su-30MKK

By contrast, the 'Komsomolsk Su-30' is manufactured by KnAAPO and started with the Su-30MKK made for China. Su-30s from KnAAPO are based on a standard Su-27U airframe, albeit strengthened for heavier payloads, and closed-architecture fire-control system, although successive upgrades have been incorporated. Confusingly, both lines are referred to as Su-30s. The largest user of the Su-30 is India, with nearly 300 aircraft.

FIGHTER AIRCRAFT

# Sukhoi Su-33 'Flanker-D' and Shenyang J-15

> The carrier Flanker was developed just before the end of the Soviet Union, and 20 years later a much modernized version was put into production by China.

The Su-33 differs most obviously from its land-based brethren in its use of canard foreplanes. These serve to reduce the angle of attack for take-off and landing and the aircraft is also equipped with an arrester hook and strengthened undercarriage with twin nosewheels. Modifications for carrier use were made to the flight-control system and the aircraft features a greater use of anti-corrosion materials,

A Russian Navy Su-33 launches from the aircraft carrier *Admiral Kuznetsov*.

## Sukhoi Su-33 'Flanker-D'

**Weight (maximum take-off):** 24,500kg (54,013lb)
**Dimensions:** Length 21.2m (69ft 6in) without probe, Wingspan 14.7m (48ft 3in), Height 5.72m (18ft 9in)
**Powerplant:** Two modified AL-31F series 3 turbofans, each rated at 122.5kN (27,558lb) with afterburning

**Maximum speed:** Mach 2.17, 2680km/h (1665mph)
**Range:** 3000km (1864 miles)
**Ceiling:** 17,000m (55,775ft)
**Crew:** 1
**Armament:** One GSh-301 30mm (1.2in) cannon; up to 6500kg (14,330lb) of stores carried on 12 hardpoints

# FIGHTER AIRCRAFT

**All images:**
Deployed aboard the carrier Kuznetsov during its initial cruise in 1996, '64 Red' was one of 13 Su-33s operating from the vessel. The canard foreplanes are an obvious distinguishing feature of the Su-33 as no other single-seat 'Flanker' currently in service possesses these control surfaces.

including in its engines. A folding mechanism is incorporated in the outer wing panels, tailplanes, radome and tailboom to ease shipboard stowage and an inflight refuelling probe is included on the port side of the nose with provision for a buddy refuelling pod to be fitted under the fuselage. After Soviet carrier trials in 1989, the Su-33 entered service with the Russian Navy in 1998, and as of 2025 around 14 examples are in service.

## Shenyang J-15

China purchased one of the development airframes in 2004 and this has been used in conjunction with the Chinese-built Flanker, the J-11, as the basis for its own shipborne fighter, the J-15. By 2025 the Chinese Navy reportedly had around 60 J-15s in service.

FIGHTER AIRCRAFT

# Sukhoi Su-35 'Flanker-E/M'

A much updated fighter derived from the Sukhoi Su-27 airframe, the Su-35 has been acquired by Russia as a lower-cost aircraft to supplement the Su-57.

Compared to the Su-27, the Su-35 features a revised aerodynamic configuration with thrust-vectoring engines and a quadruple-redundant digital fly-by-wire system for enhanced agility, shorter fins with wider rudders, a shorter tail 'sting' containing an N012 rearward-looking radar, and the deletion of the large dorsal airbrake. The airframe structure makes greater use of composite materials for lower

Finished in the darker gunship grey that is standard on later Flankers, this Su-35 was photographed at the MAKS 2015 air show.

### Sukhoi Su-35S Flanker-M

**Weight (maximum take-off):** 34,500kg (76,059lb)
**Dimensions:** Length 21.9m (71ft 10in), Wingspan 14.7m (48ft 2in), Height 5.9m (19ft 4in)
**Powerplant:** Two thrust-vectoring Saturn AL-41F-1S (izdeliye 117S) turbofans, each rated at 86.29kN (19,400lbf) dry and 137.29kN (30,865lbf) with afterburning

**Maximum speed:** 2400km/h (1500mph)
**Range:** 3600km (2200 miles)
**Ceiling:** 18,000m (59,055ft)
**Crew:** 1
**Armament:** One 30mm (1.2in) Gryazev-Shipunov GSh-30-1 autocannon; up to 8000kg (17,637lb) of weapons and stores on 12 hardpoints

## FIGHTER AIRCRAFT

**Above:**
Russian Air Force Su-35S '08 Red' is depicted as it was demonstrated in November 2014 at 'Airshow China 10' at Zhuhai Jinwan Airport.

**Opposite top:**
Depicted as it was seen while escorting a Xian H-6K bomber over the Bashi Channel, Philippines, in May 2018, this PLAAF Su-35, 'Yellow 22', is armed with Vympel R-73 (AA-11 Archer) air-to-ship and R-27 (AA-10 Alamo-A) air-to-air underwing missiles.

**Above:**
'52 Red' is an Su-35S that was displayed at the MAKS 2019 air show. This aircraft had previously been used to perform strikes on Syrian targets in support of forces loyal to President Assad.

weight and the Irbis passive electronically scanned array radar, reported to be capable of detecting hostile aircraft at a range of 400km (882 miles), was introduced as part of a revised fire-control system.

### Ukraine war

The first Su-35S was delivered to the air force in late 2011 and Russia's Su-35 fleet stands at around 110 aircraft in 2025. The aircraft has been active over Ukraine and is credited with eight air-to-air victories since 2022 but five have been reported lost, though none in aerial combat. Export customers for the Su-35 so far include China, which has taken delivery of 24 aircraft, and Iran, which has ordered 50. Indonesia reportedly ordered the type in 2018 but by 2025 no deliveries had been made.

FIGHTER AIRCRAFT

# Sukhoi Su-57 'Felon'

> Although the development of Russia's response to the F-22 proved difficult, the fifth-generation Su-57 is clearly a formidable design featuring low observability and supercruise capability.

Developed in conjunction with India, the Su-57 eventually became a purely Russian programme following India's decision to withdraw in 2018 due to concerns over cost and the aircraft not meeting India's performance requirements. The prototype had flown in 2010 but a variety of factors, including Western sanctions, the downturn of the Russian economy, structural issues and the loss of one of

An Su-57 displays its distinctive 'pixel' camouflage during a demonstration flight at the MAKS 2019 air show.

### Sukhoi Su-57

**Weight (maximum take-off):** 35,000kg (77,162lb)
**Dimensions:** Length 20.1m (66ft), Wingspan 14.1m (46ft 3in), Height 4.6m (15ft 1in)
**Powerplant:** Two Saturn AL-41F1 thrust-vectoring turbofans, each rated at 147.2kN (33,100lb) thrust with afterburning

**Maximum speed:** Mach 2.0, 2470km/h (1535mph)
**Range:** 3500km (2175 miles)
**Ceiling:** 20,000m (65,617ft)
**Crew:** 1
**Armament:** One GSh-301 30mm (1.2in) cannon, plus disposable ordnance carried in the lower fuselage

FIGHTER AIRCRAFT

**Above:**
The ninth prototype of the Su-57, '509 Blue' was first flown on 24 April 2017. The Su-57's poor rear hemisphere stealth is expected to be improved with a new exhaust nozzle.

**Opposite top:**
Although bearing the serial number 01, this Su-57 is actually the second full production machine, which was renumbered following the crash of the first example in December 2019.

**Above:**
From the front, the boat-hull-like fuselage and underslung air intakes are apparent. It is believed that blockers shield the engine's compressor face (a prime reflecting surface) from detection by radar.

the first pre-production aircraft as it was being delivered, delayed service entry of the Su-57 until December 2021.

## Limited service

Just under 30 production aircraft had been delivered to the Russian Aerospace Forces by the end of 2024 of an intended total of 76 and the aircraft has seen service over Syria and Ukraine. Unconfirmed Russian sources claim that a Ukrainian Su-27 has been destroyed by the Su-57 in combat. No Su-57s have yet been exported, though Algeria has ordered 14 examples of the type and Vietnam has announced its intention to purchase the aircraft as well.

# Attack, Bomber & Anti-Submarine Aircraft

Historically, air forces have tended to neglect the ground attack and close support role, tending to focus on the more glamorous realm of fighter aircraft. Yet recent conflicts have served to demonstrate that tactical missions of this kind are required near constantly, whereas air combat takes place comparatively rarely. By contrast the strategic bomber, able to traverse large distances with a heavy bombload, is a hangover from the Cold War – and aircraft like the Boeing B-52 are still proving highly useful.

**Opposite: A German air force PA-200 Tornado fighter taxis prior to taking off for the F-16 and Tornado 50th anniversary celebration flyover at Spangdahlem Air Base, Germany, May 2024.**

ATTACK, BOMBER, & ANTI-SUBMARINE AIRCRAFT

# Aermacchi M-346 Master/ Yakovlev Yak-130 'Mitten'

Two iterations of the same basic design, the M-346 and Yak-130, were co-developed in the 1990s as modern lead-in trainers, and both entered service in the 2010s.

Development of this trainer and light attack aircraft was begun by Yakovlev while the USSR was still in existence but the collapse of the Soviet Union compelled the design bureau to seek an international partner to develop the aircraft. Consequently, in 1992, Aermacchi joined Yakovlev to collaboratively develop the aircraft with the Italian company responsible for the project's financial and technical support.

A Yak-130 RF-81681 takes off during the Victory Day parade rehearsal at Kubinka air force base, 2017.

## Yakovlev Yak-130 'Mitten'

**Weight (maximum take-off):** 10,290kg (22,679lb)
**Dimensions:** Length 11.49m (37ft 9in), Wingspan 9.84m (32ft 3in), Height 4.76m (15ft 7in)
**Powerplant:** Two Ukrainian Progress/Zaporizhzhya AI-222-25 turbofans, each rated at 24.5kN (5510lbf)

**Maximum speed:** 1060km/h (659 miles)
**Range:** 1600km (994 miles)
**Ceiling:** 12,500m (41,013ft)
**Crew:** 2
**Armament:** Up to 3000kg (6614lb) weapons and stores on nine hardpoints

## ATTACK, BOMBER, & ANTI-SUBMARINE AIRCRAFT

**Opposite:**
'30 Red' is a Yak-130 that appeared at the Kubinka air display in August 2021, finished in three-tone blue-grey camouflage and fitted with a pair of external tanks.

**Below:**
Yak-130 '26 White' was part of a four-ship formation display that appeared at Zhukovsky air display in the summer of 2012.

**An Aermacchi M-346 prototype in flight.**

### Widely deployed

The prototype Yak-130 flew in 1996 but the partnership ended in 1999 and the two companies agreed to market their own developed designs to different parts of the world. Today, both the Yak-130 and M-346 have proved successful and both are operated by just under 10 nations respectively, with more orders likely in future. Externally almost identical, the major difference between the two aircraft is the engine: twin Progress AI-222s power the Yak while the Macchi features US-made ITEC F124 engines. The M-346 began training pilots for the Italian Air Force in 2015 but the Yak-130 preceded it, beginning aircrew training in 2013. To date the Yak-130 is the only one of the two that has seen combat, aircraft of the Myanmar Air Force having been used in airstrikes in the ongoing civil war since 2020.

ATTACK, BOMBER & ANTI-SUBMARINE AIRCRAFT

# Aero L-39 Albatros

> One of the world's most successful trainers, still employed in large numbers in an instructional role, the L-39 has been used on occasion in its secondary role as a light attack craft.

The L-39 made its maiden flight in November 1969 and immediately proved popular, being taken on strength by most of the Warsaw Pact nations, including the Soviet Union, to become one of the most successful Czech aircraft ever built. Popular with pilots for its pleasant flying characteristics and with operators, both military and civilian, for its relative simplicity, affordability and reliability,

Many L-39s have enjoyed a successful post-military career as private aircraft, with over 200 examples, such as this one, on the US civil register alone.

### Aero L-39 Skyfox

**Weight (maximum take-off):** 5800kg (12,787lb)
**Dimensions:** Length 11.83m (38ft 10in), Wingspan 9.37m (30ft 9in), Height 4.77m (15ft 8in)
**Powerplant:** One Williams International FJ44-4M turbofan, rated at 16.89kN (3,800lbf) thrust

**Maximum speed:** 900km/h (560mph)
**Range:** 2590km (1610 miles) on internal fuel
**Ceiling:** 11,500m (37,700ft)
**Crew:** 2
**Armament:** Up to 1640kg (3616lb) of stores on five hardpoints

## ATTACK, BOMBER, & ANTI-SUBMARINE AIRCRAFT

**All images:**
Although originally taken on strength with the Czechoslovak Air Force in 1984, this airframe was returned to manufacturer Aero Vodochody for use as a demonstrator and is shown here in the scheme it wore in this role when it was displayed at Boscombe Down Airshow in the UK in June 1990.

nearly 3000 have been produced in total and developed versions continue to be manufactured.

## Up-armed

Initially equipped with only two underwing pylons for weapons or fuel, later variants are equipped with four pylons and a hardpoint under the fuselage to which a gunpod containing a GSh-23L 23-millimetre twin-barrelled cannon can be fitted. The follow-on L-59 was produced only in small numbers but the latest variant, the L-39 Skyfox, the first prototype of which took to the sky in 2018, is powered by an American Williams FJ44 engine and has received a swathe of orders with the first customer, Vietnam, taking delivery of the first batch of aircraft in late 2023.

ATTACK, BOMBER & ANTI-SUBMARINE AIRCRAFT

# Aero L-159 ALCA

> Derived from the L-39 Albatros, the L-159 ALCA (advanced light combat aircraft) is available in both single- and two-seat form as a light multirole combat aircraft or advanced trainer.

In the mid 1990s the Czech Air Force was looking to replace a variety of Soviet designs with Czech-built aircraft. Wishing to avoid the expense of a new design, the decision was taken to utilize an Albatros derivative. The Czech government placed an order for 72 single-seat L-159As and the ALCA made its first flight on 4 August 1997. Most of the original batch of Czech L-159As

From this angle the L-159's L-39 Albatros ancestry is apparent though the longer nose and wing pylons.

### Aero L-159A ALCA

**Weight (maximum take-off):** 2340kg (5159lb)
**Dimensions:** Length 12.72m (41ft 9in), Wingspan 9.54m (31ft 4in), Height 4.87m (16ft)
**Powerplant:** One Honeywell/ITEC F124-GA-100 turbofan engine, rated at 28.2kN (6,300lbf) thrust
**Maximum speed:** 936km/h (582mph)

**Range:** 1570km (980 miles)
**Ceiling:** 13,200m (43,300ft)
**Crew:** 1
**Armament:** Up to three ZVI PL-20 Plamen gun pods, each containing two 20mm (0.79in) twin barrel autocannons; up to 2340kg (5159lb) ordnance and stores on seven hardpoints

## ATTACK, BOMBER, & ANTI-SUBMARINE AIRCRAFT

**Opposite:**
The Iraqi Air Force acquired 14 L-159s that within a year of delivery were participating in attacks against ISIL insurgents in the city of Fallujah.

**Top and above: The largest operator of the L-159 is the Czech Republic, and 16 of the fleet were upgraded in 2016. The photograph depicts a visiting Czech L-159 ALCA taxiing at Kleine Brogel Air Base in Belgium.**

was subsequently sold, with 12 going to the Iraqi Air Force. In Iraqi hands the L-159As saw combat service in attacks on positions held by Islamic State of Iraq and the Levant (ISIL) insurgents in the city of Fallujah in 2016 and then in operations against insurgents in the Hamrin mountains in 2021. Twenty-one ex-Czech aircraft were also acquired by the private contractor Draken International, which utilizes the type under contract to both the US Air Force (USAF) and Royal Air Force (RAF) as aggressor aircraft in training exercises.

Subsequent L-159 development has focused on two-seat variants of the aircraft, utilizing modified single-seaters taken out of storage. While these are intended primarily for training, they retain their full combat capability.

ATTACK, BOMBER, & ANTI-SUBMARINE AIRCRAFT

# Boeing P-8 Poseidon

> Intended to replace the venerable P-3 Orion, Boeing's P-8 Poseidon maritime patrol aircraft utilizes the airframe of the ubiquitous Boeing 737 airliner.

Winner of a competition held in 2000 to select a replacement for the Orion, the P-8 is derived from the 737-800ERX airliner but with numerous modifications to render it suitable for military use. The airframe is strengthened to allow the P-8 to operate for prolonged periods at relatively low altitudes and allow it to engage in more aggressive manoeuvring than any commercial

A US Navy P-8A Poseidon aircraft from Patrol Squadron (VP) 16 flies over Naval Air Station Jacksonville.

### Boeing P-8A Poseidon

**Weight (maximum take-off):** 85,820kg (189,200lb)
**Dimensions:** Length 39.47m (129ft 5in), Wingspan 37.64m (123ft 6in), Height 12.83m (42ft 1in)
**Powerplant:** Two CFM International F108 turbofans 121kN (27,300lbf)

**Maximum speed:** 907km/h (564mph)
**Range:** 2225km (1383 miles) with four hours on station
**Ceiling:** 12,500m (41,000ft)
**Crew:** Flight crew 2, mission crew 7
**Armament:** Up to 5670kg (12,700lbs) of ordnance in weapons bay

ATTACK, BOMBER, & ANTI-SUBMARINE AIRCRAFT

**Opposite:**
The stylized golden eagle artwork on the tail denotes Patrol Squadron VP-9 which transitioned to the P-8 after operating the P-3 Orion for 54 years.

**Above (both images):**
This P-8A serves with another long-standing P-3 unit, VP-26, which transitioned to the P-8A in 2016, carrying out its first sorties with the new aircraft in the following year.

aircraft. As well as a near total absence of cabin windows – just two are provided for observation – the aircraft can easily be distinguished from a regular 737 by the inclusion of a weapons bay for torpedoes and other stores immediately aft of the wing.

### Export success

After making its maiden flight in April 2009, the first serial production P-8 was delivered to the US Navy in March 2012 and 118 Poseidons were in service by 2025. The fact that the P-8 is based on the well-known 737 makes it an attractive export prospect and the aircraft has been delivered to several nations since the early 2020s with Australia, Canada, Germany, India, New Zealand, Norway, South Korea and the UK all ordering the type. More are likely to be procured by other nations in the future.

ATTACK, BOMBER, & ANTI-SUBMARINE AIRCRAFT

# Boeing B-52 Stratofortress

One of military aviation's great survivors, the veteran B-52 is not expected to retire until the mid 2050s, a full century after it entered US Air Force (USAF) service in 1955.

One of the most iconic aircraft of the Cold War, the B-52 achieved 70 years of continuous service in 2025 and although designed as a nuclear bomber, it has only ever dropped conventional munitions in combat. The eight-turbojet swept-wing XB-52 first flew in April 1952. 744 B-52s were built, the last, a B-52H, leaving the factory in 1962, but the aircraft has been kept viable through the

Typically smoky departure as a B-52 Stratofortress takes off from a forward operating location in South West Asia, 2006.

### Boeing B-52 Stratofortress

**Weight (maximum take-off):** 221,323kg (488,000lb)
**Dimensions:** Length 48.5m (159ft 4in), Wingspan 56.4m (185ft), Height 12.4m (40ft 8in)
**Powerplant:** Eight Pratt & Whitney TF33-P-3/103 turbofans, each rated at 7750kg (17,000lb) thrust

**Maximum speed:** 1050kmh (650mph)
**Range:** 14,200km (8800 miles)
**Ceiling:** 15,000m (50,000ft)
**Crew:** 5
**Armament:** Up to 32,000kg (70,548lb) of ordnance, including AGM-84, AGM-142 and AGM-86C missiles, JSOW and JDAM bombs

## ATTACK, BOMBER, & ANTI-SUBMARINE AIRCRAFT

**Opposite:**
B-52H of the 2nd Bomb Wing's 11th Bomb Squadron based at Barksdale Air Force Base in Louisiana. The 2nd BW has operated B-52s from this location for over 60 years.

**Above:**
The blue and gold checkered stripe and BD tailcode reveal this B-52H is on the strength of the 93rd Bomb Squadron, the Air Force's B-52 Formal Training Unit.

**Right:**
Today the Stratofortress fleet flies in overall grey but during the Vietnam war B-52 upper surfaces were camouflaged in SEA (South East Asia) colours. Undersides were gloss black.

application of various system and equipment upgrades. The latest sees an engine change to the Rolls-Royce F130 to become the B-52J with conversion expected to take place during the 2020s.

### Nuclear bomber

The B-52's career saw it drop the world's first air-dropped thermonuclear weapon at Bikini Atoll in 1956 before serving throughout the Vietnam war, dropping tens of thousands of tons of bombs on Hanoi and other targets. B-52s were also on permanent 24-hour alert as part of the US nuclear deterrent until 1991. By 2025, the B-52's range and comparative economy of operation make it an attractive choice when attacking targets unlikely to be protected by sophisticated defences, and in 2025 76 B-52Hs remained in active service.

ATTACK, BOMBER, & ANTI-SUBMARINE AIRCRAFT

# Dassault/Dornier Alpha Jet

**In the 1970s, France and Germany collaborated to produce the Alpha Jet, intended as both a trainer and for close support. Considerable numbers of the Alpha Jet remain in service.**

First flown in October 1973, the Alpha Jet was produced in two distinct lines: the Alpha Jet E, with E standing for *Ecole* ('School'), optimized for the training role, which was the primary function France required from the type, and the Alpha Jet A, with A standing for *Appui Tactique* ('Tactical Support') for ground attack. The latter role was of primary interest to the Germans, though the Luftwaffe

A French Air Force Alpha Jet E taxies in at Mont-de-Marsan Air Base in May 2019.

### Alpha Jet A

**Weight (maximum take-off):** 7500kg (16,535lb)
**Dimensions:** Length 13.23m (43ft 5in), Wingspan: 9.11m (29ft 11in), Height: 4.19m (13ft 9in)
**Powerplant:** Two SNECMA Turbomeca Larzac 04-C5 turbofan engines, each rated at 13.24kN (2,980lbf) thrust

**Maximum speed:** 1000km/h (620mph)
**Range:** 2940km (1830 miles) ferry range with drop tanks
**Ceiling:** 4630m (48,000ft)
**Crew:** 2
**Armament:** One 27mm (1.06in) Mauser BK-27 cannon or one 30mm (1.18in) DEFA cannon; up to 2500kg (5512lb) ordnance and fuel

## ATTACK, BOMBER, & ANTI-SUBMARINE AIRCRAFT

**All images:**
Belgium was one of many export customers for the Alpha Jet where the aircraft replaced the Fouga Magister in the training role. Belgium withdrew its fleet in 2019, selling 25 airframes and spares to the Canadian Top Aces company.

also employed a number of Portugal-based Alpha Jet As for weapons training. Germany retired its Alpha Jets in the 1990s and sold its fleet to Portugal and Thailand, the latter nation operating the type until the present day. Some German examples were acquired by the private company Top Aces, which owns 60 airframes, though not all are airworthy, and utilizes them for various government training programmes in Canada.

### French service

France still operates the Alpha Jet E as a lead-in trainer and all other nations that retain the type operate Alpha Jet Es, notably Nigeria which employs the type as an armed combat aircraft and which has conducted multiple Alpha Jet air strikes against Boko Haram militants since 2014.

ATTACK, BOMBER, & ANTI-SUBMARINE AIRCRAFT

# Embraer EMB 312 Tucano and EMB 314 Super Tucano

> One of the Brazilian Embraer company's first international successes, the Tucano was used by many nations and continues to be produced in updated Super Tucano form.

The Tucano owes its existence to a Brazilian requirement to produce a more fuel-efficient trainer in the wake of the mid 1970s fuel crisis as a replacement for the Cessna T-37. The EMB 312 was modified from a 1977 Counter-Insurgency (COIN) design drawn up by Embraer's chief designer Josef Kovács.

The prototype flew for the first time in August 1980 and the first of

This Indonesian Air Force EMB 314 was photographed landing at Malta during its 2016 delivery flight from Brazil.

### Embraer EMB 314 Super Tucano

**Weight (maximum take-off):** 5400kg (11,905lb)
**Dimensions:** Length 1.38m (37ft 4in), Wingspan 11.14m (36ft 7in), Height 3.97m (13ft 0in)
**Powerplant:** One 1196kW (1604hp) Pratt & Whitney Canada PT6A-68C turboprop engine
**Maximum speed:** 590km/h (370mph)

**Range:** 1330km (830 miles)
**Ceiling:** 10,668m (35,000ft)
**Crew:** 1 or 2
**Armament:** Two 12.7mm (0.5in) FN Herstal or US Ordnance M3P machine guns as fixed forward firing in wings; up to 1550kg (3300lb) of ordnance, gun pods or fuel on five hardpoints

ATTACK, BOMBER, & ANTI-SUBMARINE AIRCRAFT

**Opposite:**
A Tucano utilized by the 'Esquadrilha da Fumaca' (Smoke Squadron) display team. The team's aircraft were replaced with the Super Tucano in 2013.

**Above (both images):**
The Super Tucano has seen considerable combat since its introduction, for example undertaking thousands of air strikes against the Taliban in Afghan Air Force hands. Brazilian air force A-29Bs like this one have been utilized to intercept drug-running aircraft and bomb illicit airstrips in the Amazon.

an eventual 168 examples acquired by the Brazilian Air Force was delivered in 1983. These were produced in two variants, the T-27 trainer and AT-27 light attack aircraft, and the Tucano also equipped 13 other air forces. Most operators were South American but Angola, Egypt, Mauritania and France all adopted the type as well, and the UK licence-built 160 examples of a modified version, the Short Tucano.

## New airframe
Further development resulted in the EMB 314 Super Tucano with a strengthened airframe, cockpit pressurization and stretched fuselage housing the more powerful PT6A-68C engine. Flown in 1999 and in production ever since, the Super Tucano has proved even more successful than its predecessor, operating with over 20 nations as a trainer and including the USA which designated it the A-29.

ATTACK, BOMBER, & ANTI-SUBMARINE AIRCRAFT

# Fairchild A-10 Thunderbolt II

> The unique A-10 was unlike any aircraft that had come before. Now reaching the end of its long service life, its intended replacement with the F-35 has caused some controversy.

Designed uncompromisingly for ground attack, the A-10's unusual design was dictated by its primary armament, the enormous 30mm (1.18in) GAU-8 Avenger rotary autocannon, in combination with the desire to make the aircraft as resistant to battle damage as possible. The pilot and some systems are encased in an armoured titanium 'bathtub' weighing 540kg (1200lb) and the A-10

An A-10C of the Thunderbolt II Demonstration Team flies over the Skyfest air show at the appropriately named Fairchild Air Force Base in June 2024.

### Fairchild A-10C

**Weight (maximum take-off):** 20,865kg (46,000lb)
**Dimensions:** Length 16.26m (53ft 4in), Wingspan 17.53m (57ft 6in), Height 4.47m (14ft 8in)
**Powerplant:** Two General Electric TF34-GE-100A turbofans, each rated at 40.32kN (9,065lbf) thrust

**Maximum speed:** 706km/h (439mph)
**Range:** 4,150km (2580 miles) ferry range with maximum fuel
**Ceiling:** 13,700m (45,000ft)
**Crew:** 1
**Armament:** One 30mm (1.18in) GAU-8/A Avenger rotary cannon; up to 7,260kg (16,000lb) ordanance and fuel on 11 hardpoints

124

## ATTACK, BOMBER, & ANTI-SUBMARINE AIRCRAFT

**Opposite:**
Then serving with the 10th Tactical Fighter Wing, this A-10A was based at RAF Alconbury in the UK in 1990.

**Above:**
Although identical to standard A-10, those aircraft utilized for Forward-Air-Control (FAC) duties were designated the OA-10. This OA-10A carries the 'PA' tailcode of the 103rd Fighter Squadron, 11th Fighter Group, of the Pennsylvania Air National Guard.

**Below:**
The A-10C is still flown by the 104th Fighter Squadron. Today all A-10s are standardly finished in this all-over grey scheme.

is designed to be able to fly with one engine, half of the tail, one elevator and half of a wing missing.

The aircraft entered service in 1976 and were first actively deployed during the US invasion of Grenada in 1983 but did not fire a shot in anger until 1991's Operation Desert Storm where they were heavily committed and proved highly successful, then seeing further active service in Yugoslavia, the second Gulf War and Afghanistan.

## In service today

In total, 261 A-10s remain in service in 2025. The aircraft is officially due for retirement by the end of the 2020s but debate continues about whether this should go ahead as the F-35 is perceived as too expensive and potentially less effective in the close support role.

ATTACK, BOMBER, & ANTI-SUBMARINE AIRCRAFT

# Hongdu JL-8/Karakorum K-8

> A joint venture between China and Pakistan, the JL-8/K-8 is a successful trainer and light attack aircraft that has been widely exported and used in combat operations by Myanmar.

Developed in the mid 1980s, the JL-8 was intended to replace such ageing aircraft as the JJ-5 (a trainer variant of the venerable MiG-17) in Chinese service, whereas the Pakistan Air Force wanted an intermediate trainer to replace the T-37 Tweet. Flying for the first time in November 1990, the People's Liberation Army Air Force (PLAAF) received its first JL-8s in 1992 with Pakistan taking delivery of its first

Colourful Hongdu JL-8 trainer aircraft on static display prior to the Changchun Airshow in August 2022.

## Karakorum K-8

**Weight (maximum take-off):** 4330kg (9546lb)
**Dimensions:** Length 11.6m (38ft 1in), Wingspan 9.63m (31ft 7 in), Height 4.1m (13ft 5in)
**Powerplant:** One Honeywell TFE731-2A turbofan, rated at 16.01kN (3600lbf) thrust
**Maximum speed:** 800km/h (500mph)

**Range:** 2250km (1400 miles)
**Ceiling:** 13,000m (43,000ft)
**Crew:** 2
**Armament:** One optional 23mm (0.9in) cannon pod (mounted on centreline hardpoint), up to 1000kg (2205lb) ordnance and fuel on five hardpoints

ATTACK, BOMBER, & ANTI-SUBMARINE AIRCRAFT

**Opposite:**
This Chinese PLAAF JL-8 appeared at Zhuhai Jinwan Airshow in 2016. Since its introduction the JL-8's affordability has resulted in considerable export interest.

**Above & left:**
In more typical service finish, this JL-8 is one of around 350 in service with the PLAAF. Export aircraft utilize a US Honeywell engine but domestic Chinese aircraft feature a Chinese-manufactured version of the Ukrainian Ivchenko AI-25 (DV-2) engine, designated WS-11.

Karakorum K-8s in 1994. The aircraft is named after the Karakorum mountains that form the China–Pakistan border and was chosen to represent the goodwill between the two nations. Chinese aircraft are powered by the WS-11, a Chinese-built version of the Ukrainian Ivchenko AI-25, but the K-8 features the American Honeywell TFE731-2A turbofan.

## Affordable trainer

After appearing at the Singapore Airshow in 1993, the aircraft was marketed as an affordable trainer with low maintenance requirements that could be rapidly reconfigured as a multirole combat aircraft. The K-8 has enjoyed some success on the world market with 13 other nations taking delivery of the type, mostly for training use, but Bolivia has acquired the K-8 for use in anti-drug operations and Myanmar has used the K-8 in combat against Kachin independence fighters. Over 500 have been built and the type remains in production.

ATTACK, BOMBER, & ANTI-SUBMARINE AIRCRAFT

# Hongdu JL-10 and L-15

> The JL-10 was developed to meet the advanced trainer requirements of both the Chinese Air Force and Navy and is also capable of operating as a light attack aircraft.

Flying for the first time in 2006, the JL-10 was in competition with the cheaper and somewhat simpler JL-9 for the advanced trainer role, a competition it subsequently won. Hongdu had consulted with the Yakovlev design bureau during the aircraft's development, and it is probably no coincidence that the JL-10 closely resembles the Yak-130. It is also powered by the same engines

A Hongdu JL-10 releases flares as part of its display during the China Aviation Industry Conference and Nanchang Air Show, 2022.

### Hongdu JL-10B

**Weight (maximum take-off):** 11,600kg (25,574lb)
**Dimensions:** Length 12.4m (40ft 8in), Wingspan 9.4m (30ft 10in), Height 4.7m (15ft 5in)
**Powerplant:** Two Ivchenko-Progress AI-222K-25F afterburning turbofan engines, each rated at 24.7kN (5,553lbf) dry, 41.2kN (9,262lbf) with afterburner

**Maximum speed:** 1729km/h (1074mph)
**Range:** 2600km (1600 miles) ferry range with maximum fuel
**Ceiling:** 16,000m (52,000ft)
**Crew:** 2
**Armament:** Up to 3500kg (7716lb) of ordnance and fuel on nine hardpoints

## ATTACK, BOMBER, & ANTI-SUBMARINE AIRCRAFT

**Right: The planform resemblance between the Yak-130/M-346 and the JL-10 is evident. Around 65 JL-10s are believed to have been delivered to the Chinese PLAAF and Navy by 2025.**

**Opposite & right:** This JL-10, serial number 2510, was observed at Changchun Dafangshen Air Base in October 2019.

as the Russian aircraft. Service entry of the base JL-10 is believed to have occurred during 2013 with the People's Liberation Army Air Force (PLAAF).

### Supersonic version

The L-15B, which first flew in December 2017, is a supersonic development intended for lead-in fighter training (LIFT) and has reportedly been in service since 2019. Compared to the less sophisticated JL-9, the L-15B reduces conversion training time as it is more representative of the most recent PLAAF fighter types.

The L-15 is also being offered for export and examples have been delivered to Zambia in 2017 and the UAE, which received its first L-15Bs in late 2023.

129

ATTACK, BOMBER, & ANTI-SUBMARINE AIRCRAFT

# Ilyushin Il-38 'May'

Based on the Il-18 airliner of 1957, the Il-38 is a shore-based anti-submarine warfare (ASW) aircraft, with secondary maritime patrol and surveillance roles.

Making its first flight in 1967, the Il-38 entered Soviet Naval Aviation service in 1969 and ultimately 65 Il-38s were built, including a handful of the maritime search and rescue (MSAR) variant that carried a parachutable rescue pod semi-externally in the forward weapons bay. On the standard ASW Il-38, the forward bay contained sonobuoys and the rear one held mines, homing torpedoes and depth

This Russian Navy Il-38N was photographed in 2019. The boxy strut mounted fairing above the cockpit houses ELINT equipment.

### Ilyushin Il-38

**Weight (maximum take-off):** 66,000kg (145,505lb)
**Dimensions:** Length 40.14m (131ft 8in), Wingspan 37.42m (122ft 9in), Height 10.17m (33ft 4in)
**Powerplant:** Four 3169ekW (4250ehp) Ivchenko Progress AI-20M turboprops

**Maximum speed:** 650km/h (404mph)
**Range:** 6500km (4039 miles)
**Ceiling:** 11,000m (36,089ft)
**Crew:** 7–8
**Armament:** Up to 8400kg (18,519lb) weapons and stores

ATTACK, BOMBER, & ANTI-SUBMARINE AIRCRAFT

**Opposite:**
In Soviet service, Il-38s wore only a small identifying number on an otherwise all-grey airframe.

**Above:**
This Russian Navy Il-38 of the Navy Training Regiment at Ostrov airvbase was much photographed in the West due to its appearance at the Royal International Air Tattoo at Fairford, UK, in 1996.

**Below:**
India operated seven Il-38s for around four decades but withdrew the type in 2023.

charges, both conventional and nuclear. A change in the centre of gravity of the aircraft resulted in the entire wing being moved forward approximately 3m (10ft) compared with the standard Il-18. It was also fitted with a prominent MAD boom at the tail, and a radome for the search and targeting system was mounted ventrally just behind the nosegear.

### Sturdy flyer

Il-38s were popular with their crews, proving reliable and safe and possessing pleasant handling characteristics. Most served with the Soviet Union but five were supplied to India, though these were retired in 2023. The avionics and sensory equipment of the fleet has been significantly upgraded over the last five decades and Russia continues to operate the type in the ASW role.

ATTACK, BOMBER, & ANTI-SUBMARINE AIRCRAFT

# Kawasaki P-1

Unique among modern maritime patrol aircraft in that it is a clean sheet design, not a converted airliner, the Japanese Maritime Self-Defence Force (JMSDF) took delivery of its first P-1 in 2013.

Looking for a replacement for its P-3C Orion maritime patrol craft, the JMSDF found that no existing type fully met its requirements and so work began on producing a purpose-built indigenous aircraft. The P-X project was launched in 2001 with Kawasaki as prime contractor and, to save development costs and time, it was decided to use some major components developed for the C-2 transport aircraft, including the outer wings, horizontal tailplane

A striking contrast to the blue-grey production machines that followed, the prototype P-1 was finished in this attractive red and white scheme.

## Kawasaki P-1

**Weight (maximum take-off):** 79,700kg (175,708lb)
**Dimensions:** Length 38m (124ft 8in), Wingspan 35.4m (116ft 2in), Height 12.1m (39ft 8in)
**Powerplant:** Four IHI Corporation F7 turbofan engines, each rated at 60kN (13,000lbf) thrust
**Maximum speed:** 996km/h (619mph)

**Range:** 8000km (5000 miles)
**Ceiling:** 13,520m (44,360ft)
**Crew:** Flight crew 3, mission crew 8
**Armament:** Up to 9,000kg (19,842lb) in bomb bay and eight external hardpoints

## ATTACK, BOMBER, & ANTI-SUBMARINE AIRCRAFT

**Opposite & above:** The large cockpit windows belie the considerable size of the P-1. Kawasaki pushed hard to find international buyers for the P-1 and it became the first Japanese military aircraft to visit a European air show when a P-1 attended the 2015 Royal International Air Tattoo in the UK in an attempt to garner sales.

A P-1 cruises past Mt Fuji in formation with the aircraft it was designed to replace, the P-3 Orion.

and cockpit windows. Additionally, many of the internal systems are shared between the two aircraft but the IHI F7 turbofan engines were specifically designed to power the P-1.

The P-1 made its first flight on 28 September 2007 and the type was introduced to service in 2013. Almost immediately, the P-1 was being marketed to other nations as an alternative to the Boeing P-8 Poseidon, and while it is true that the P-1, purpose built for the maritime role, is a more capable aircraft, featuring a larger weapons bay and possessing greater range than the P-8, it is, crucially, more expensive. By 2025 no export sales had been made though the aircraft was still being offered to potential operators.

ATTACK, BOMBER, & ANTI-SUBMARINE AIRCRAFT

# Lockheed F-117 Night Hawk

The 'stealth fighter' was the first operational aircraft to be built incorporating stealth technology and its existence was denied for the first five years of its operational service.

Intended to minimize the aircraft's radar signature, the F-117's faceted shape, comprising multiple flat surfaces, arose due to the limited ability of 1970s computers to model radar returns from complicated shapes. Later stealth designs benefitted from more powerful computers allowing curved surfaces to be modelled accurately and so the striking appearance of the F-117

An F-117 Nighthawk flies over the Persian Gulf in 2003. The 'stealth fighter' became famous for its role in the first Gulf War.

### Lockheed F-117A Night Hawk

**Weight (maximum take-off):** 23,814kg (52,500lb)
**Dimensions:** Length 20.09m (65ft 11in), Wingspan 13.21m (43ft 4in), Height 3.78m (12ft 5in)
**Powerplant:** Two General Electric F404-GE-F1D2 turbofans, each rated at 4899kg (10,800lb) thrust
**Maximum speed:** 1100km/h (684mph)
**Range:** 1720km (1070 miles)
**Ceiling:** 14,000m (45,000ft)
**Crew:** 1
**Armament:** Up to 2268kg (5000lb) of munitions on rotary dispenser in weapons bay

ATTACK, BOMBER, & ANTI-SUBMARINE AIRCRAFT

**Opposite:**
This F-117A was flown by the commander of the 37th Tactical Fighter Wing between 1989 and 1992.

**All images (this page):**
Production machines feature a uniform finish of radar-absorbent material. This aircraft served the 49th Tactical Fighter Wing which flew the Nighthawk between 1992 and 2008.

will probably remain unique. Following the successful testing of two proof-of-concept aircraft, codenamed 'Have Blue', the decision was made to build an operational stealth aircraft under the codename 'Senior Trend'.

## Widespread service

In total 64 F-117s were built, first seeing combat during the Gulf War in 1991. Operations continued over Yugoslavia, where despite its vaunted stealth characteristics, one example was acquired by a fire control radar and shot down with a surface-to-air missile. The F-117 was also used in early airstrikes in Afghanistan. Despite being officially retired in 2007, the F-117 has actually continued to serve with the US Air Force (USAF), which maintains a fleet of around 45 aircraft. As well as performing as a stealthy aggressor for training purposes and on various trials and research programmes, the aircraft has been covertly deployed overseas, a fact revealed when an F-117 had to make an emergency landing in Kuwait in 2016.

ATTACK, BOMBER, & ANTI-SUBMARINE AIRCRAFT

# Lockheed P-3 Orion

> A Cold War workhorse, the Orion has been monitoring the world's oceans since the early 1960s. Over 60 years later, the Orion remains in large-scale service with 13 nations.

The first prototype Orion, which flew in November 1959, consisted of a converted Electra airliner. However, the P-3 would far outstrip the success of its immediate ancestor, with many Orions in service in 2025, while the Electra had stopped carrying fare-paying passengers around 30 years earlier. The US Navy began operating the P-3 in 1962, utilizing the aircraft primarily to localize Soviet submarines

A US Navy P-3C attached to VP-4, the 'Skinny Dragons', conducts a fly by of destroyer USS Cole in 2014.

## Lockheed P-3C Orion

**Weight (maximum take-off):** 64,410kg (142,000lb)
**Dimensions:** Length 35.61m (116ft 10in), Wingspan 30.37m (99ft 8in), Height 10.29m (33ft 9in)
**Powerplant:** Four 3661kW (4910hp) Allison T56-A-14 turboprops

**Maximum speed:** 761km/h (473mph)
**Range:** 3835km (2383 miles)
**Ceiling:** 8625m (28,300ft)
**Crew:** 11
**Armament:** Up to 8735kg (19,250lb) of ASW munitions

## ATTACK, BOMBER, & ANTI-SUBMARINE AIRCRAFT

**All images:**
Another VP-4 P-3C, this Orion wears the light grey scheme and low-visibility markings typical of the P-3's later USN career. VP-4 flew the P-3 from 1966 to 2017 before transitioning to the P-8 Poseidon.

detected by undersea surveillance systems and eliminate them in the event of full-scale war. Subsequently, electronic intelligence (ELINT), reconnaissance and battlespace surveillance versions of the P-3 were also operated by the US Navy and over 40 different variants were used by the US over the type's service life.

**Top endurance**
The aircraft possessed remarkable endurance, which was regularly increased by shutting down one or more of the engines. The record for the longest duration P-3 mission was set in 1972 by an RNZAF Orion which remained aloft for 21.5 hours. Ultimately replaced by the P-8 Poseidon in the US, large numbers of Orions continue to serve elsewhere, with Japan and Canada maintaining the largest operational fleets.

ATTACK, BOMBER, & ANTI-SUBMARINE AIRCRAFT

# Northrop B-2 Spirit

Highly advanced and colossally expensive, the pioneering B-2 'stealth bomber' was astonishingly radical when its existence was released to the public in November 1988.

Despite the science-fiction quality of its appearance, the B-2 was, in a sense, the culmination of over 50 years of work: Jack Northrop had dreamed of building flying wing aircraft and several experimental flying-wing bombers were flown in the immediate postwar period, the B-35 and jet-powered B-49. Control problems had scuppered the original flying wings but digital control systems

The unmistakable outline of the B-2, pictured here in flight over the Mojave Desert in California.

### Northrop B-2A Spirit

**Weight (maximum take-off):** 170,600kg (376,000lb)
**Dimensions:** Length 21.03m (69ft 0in), Wingspan 52.43m (172ft 0in), Height 5.18m (17ft 0in)
**Powerplant:** Four General Electric F118-GE-100 turbofans, each rated at 84.52kN (19,000lb) thrust

**Maximum speed:** 1010km/h (630mph)
**Range:** 11,000km (6900 miles)
**Ceiling:** 15,240m (50,000ft)
**Crew:** 2
**Armament:** Up to 18,144kg (40,000lb) of disposable stores carried in two weapons bays in underside of centre section

# ATTACK, BOMBER, & ANTI-SUBMARINE AIRCRAFT

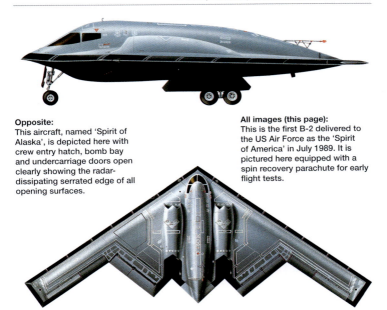

**Opposite:**
This aircraft, named 'Spirit of Alaska', is depicted here with crew entry hatch, bomb bay and undercarriage doors open clearly showing the radar-dissipating serrated edge of all opening surfaces.

**All images (this page):**
This is the first B-2 delivered to the US Air Force as the 'Spirit of America' in July 1989. It is pictured here equipped with a spin recovery parachute for early flight tests.

cured those problems for the B-2. The pure wing design without a fuselage was selected as it has a small radar signature, an effect enhanced by its coating in radar absorbent materials. The engine intakes and exhausts are mounted on the top side where they are less likely to be detected from the ground, and the heat signature of the engines is minimized by mounting them deep within the aircraft's structure.

## Nuclear bomber

Intended as a nuclear bomber able to penetrate Soviet defences, today the B-2 is used primarily as a conventional bomber, though it retains its nuclear capability. The aircraft entered service in 1993 and since then has been used in Yugoslavia, the second Gulf War, in Afghanistan and more recently against Houthi rebels in Yemen. None has been lost to enemy action. Initially planned to operate until 2058, retirement of the B-2 is now scheduled for 2032, primarily due to its high operating costs.

ATTACK, BOMBER, & ANTI-SUBMARINE AIRCRAFT

# Panavia Tornado

The 'swing wing' Tornado was developed to replace several aircraft in a variety of roles, pioneering the multinational collaborations that would become a feature of Western European aircraft procurement.

In the late 1960s, officials from West Germany, the Netherlands, Belgium, Italy and Canada formed a working group to look at replacements for the F-104G Starfighter and developed specifications for a 'multirole combat aircraft' (MRCA). Britain later joined the programme though Belgium, Canada and the Netherlands left and MRCA became a tri-national project, first flying (in Germany) in

A German Air Force Panavia Tornado aircraft takes off over Bodo, Norway, in 2018.

## Panavia Tornado GR.4

**Weight (maximum take-off):** 27,951kg (61,620lb)
**Dimensions:** Length 16.72m (54ft 10in), Wingspan 8.60m (28ft 3in) swept, 13.91m (45ft 8in) unswept, Height 5.95m (19ft 6in)
**Powerplant:** Two Turbo-Union RB199-34R Mk 103 afterburning turbofans, each rated at 43.8kN (9,800lbf) thrust dry

**Maximum speed:** 2400km/h (1500mph)
**Range:** 3890km (2420 miles) ferry range with external fuel
**Ceiling:** 15,240m (50,000ft)
**Crew:** 2
**Armament:** One fixed 27mm (1.06in) Mauser BK-27 revolver cannon; up to 9000kg (19,800lb) of ordnance and fuel

## ATTACK, BOMBER, & ANTI-SUBMARINE AIRCRAFT

**Opposite:**
This German Tornado IDS aircraft is shown carrying AGM-88 HARM missiles. The aircraft wears the markings of Taktisches Luftwaffengeschwader 51 'Immelmann'.

**Above & below:**
Saudi Arabia was the only nation other than the UK to operate both the IDS and ADV (pictured) variants of the Tornado. RSAF Tornado ADVs were equivalent to the RAF's F.3 aircraft and flew 451 sorties during Operation Desert Storm.

August 1974. The initial Tornado IDS (interdictor/strike) variant entered Luftwaffe service in 1979 with the other two nations following shortly after. The Tornado also became one of the few bomber designs in history to become a fighter, the British developed ADV (air defence variant) featuring a lengthened nose for the Foxhunter radar.

### German missions

Both variants saw operational service in the Gulf War and in 1999 IDS Tornadoes undertook the first offensive missions by Luftwaffe aircraft since World War II, conducting airstrikes in the Kosovo War. Subsequently, Tornadoes from all three of the programme's nations served in Afghanistan. Although the Tornado ADV was withdrawn from service in 2012 and the Royal Air Force (RAF) retired the IDS in 2019, variants of the IDS remain in service with Germany, Italy and Saudi Arabia, the type's only export customer.

ATTACK, BOMBER, & ANTI-SUBMARINE AIRCRAFT

# Rockwell B-1 Lancer

> The only non-Russian supersonic strategic bomber, the B-1 nuclear bomber programme survived cancellation in the 1970s to become a highly capable conventional bomber.

Originally schemed in the late 1960s as a supersonic bomber with greater range than the F-111, the B-1A flew for the first time in December 1974 but the entire programme was cancelled in 1977. However, a change of government and defence strategies saw the B-1 programme restarted in modified form, essentially as a stopgap pending delivery of the B-2 stealth bomber. The new B-1B was

With fuel port open just ahead of the cockpit, this B-1B is about to commence aerial refuelling over Nevada, USA.

### Rockwell B-1B Lancer

**Weight (maximum take-off):** 216,360kg (477,000lb)
**Dimensions:** Length 44.37m (145ft 7in), Wingspan 41.95m (137ft 7in) spread, Height 10.24m (33ft 7in)
**Powerplant:** Four General Electric F101-GE-102 turbofan engines, each rated at 77.45kN (17,390lb) thrust each dry

**Maximum speed:** 1335kmh (830mph)
**Range:** 12,000km (7455 miles)
**Ceiling:** 18,000m (60,000ft)
**Crew:** 4
**Armament:** Up to 34,000kg (74,957lb) of ordnance in three bays, including AGM-154 and AGM-158 air-to-surface missiles, Mk-82 GP bombs, Mk-62 sea mines and GBU-38 JDAM

ATTACK, BOMBER, & ANTI-SUBMARINE AIRCRAFT

**Opposite:**
The ED tailcode reveals this B-1B was on the strength of the 419th Flight Test Squadron (FLTS) and is pictured during tests of the sniper targeting pod mounted on the ventral pylon.

**Above (both images):**
This is the third production B-1B and is depicted serving with the 28th Bomb Wing at Ellsworth AFB in South Dakota. This aircraft was withdrawn in 2005 and is currently displayed at Holt Heritage Airpark in Idaho.

slower than the B-1A but carried a greater payload and was more versatile than the original aircraft.

## B1-B

A second B-1 'first flight' was made when the B-1B made its maiden flight in March 1983. One hundred aircraft were built and the first example delivered to the US Air Force (USAF) in 1985. Originally designed for a nuclear payload, the B-1B fleet was modified for the conventional role following the end of the Cold War and by the end of the 1990s the aircraft carried a full array of guided and unguided munitions. All B-1Bs were assigned to Global Strike Command in 1995 and 45 remained in service at the start of 2025.

143

# SEPECAT Jaguar

A collaboration between the United Kingdom and France, the supersonic Jaguar was utilized for the close support and nuclear strike role. It remains in service in India.

The Jaguar programme began life as a project to deliver a supersonic training aircraft and light attack aircraft to replace a variety of types in both nations and led to the British Aircraft Corporation (BAC) and Breguet combining forces. Although ostensibly based on the existing Breguet Br.121 design, BAC contributed a new wing design and high-lift devices and so many changes were required to alter

A French Air Force Jaguar A/E aircraft flies over the Adriatic Sea, in support of Operation Joint Forge in April 2003.

### SEPECAT Jaguar GR.Mk.1A

**Weight (maximum take-off):** 15,700kg (34,613lb)
**Dimensions:** Length 16.83m (55ft 3in), Wingspan 8.69m (28ft 6in), Height 4.89m (16ft 1in)
**Powerplant:** Two Rolls-Royce/Turbomeca Adour Mk 102 turbofans, each rated at 22.75kN (5,110lbf) thrust dry, 32.5kN (7,300lbf) with afterburner
**Maximum speed:** 1593km/h (990mph)
**Range:** 1902km (1182 miles) ferry range
**Ceiling:** 15,240m (50,000ft)
**Crew:** 1
**Armament:** Two 30mm (1.18in) cannon; five external hardpoints for 4536kg (10,000lb) of munitions; two AAMs

## ATTACK, BOMBER, & ANTI-SUBMARINE AIRCRAFT

**Below:**
JM255 is one of India's 12 Jaguar IMs utilized in the maritime strike role. It wears the distinctive two-tone grey camouflage adopted for this mission.

**Opposite top:**
XZ364 served in Operation Granby, the British contribution to the first Gulf War, flying 47 missions during the conflict, the most of any RAF aircraft.

**Below:**
The Jaguar IS is an all-weather tactical strike, ground-attack fighter version developed for the Indian Air Force. Thirty-five were built by BAe in the UK and a further 89 in India by HAL.

the subsonic Br.121 into a supersonic attack aircraft that the Jaguar became effectively a new design.

## Combat and export

The first Jaguar made its maiden flight in September 1968 and the production aircraft entered French service in 1973 with British aircraft following a year later. French aircraft saw considerable action in various African conflicts during the 1970s and both nations operated the type in the Gulf War. Meanwhile, export customers were being sought and Ecuador, India, Nigeria and Oman all acquired the type. India was the largest export customer and also built the Jaguar under licence at HAL. Indian-built aircraft featured more powerful engines and a different and more advanced navigation system. Utilized in action in the Kargil War, Jaguars equipped six Indian squadrons in 2025.

ATTACK, BOMBER, & ANTI-SUBMARINE AIRCRAFT

# Shenyang J-6 'Farmer' and Nanchang A-5 'Fantan'

This Chinese development of the MiG-19 has largely passed out of service but numbers remain in the inventories of a selection of African and Asian nations.

The MiG-19 was the first Soviet combat aircraft capable of exceeding the speed of sound in level flight. Although its frontline service life was comparatively brief in the USSR, China became an enthusiastic operator of the type and acquired a manufacturing licence. Chinese-produced MiG-19s were designated J-6 for domestic use and the first flight by a J-6 occurred in 1959 with production aircraft entering

A Bangladeshi air force Nanchang A-5 lands at Hazrat Shahjalal International Airport.

### Nanchang Q-5D

**Weight (maximum take-off):** 11,830kg (26,081lb)
**Dimensions:** Length 15.65m (51ft 4in), Wingspan: 9.68m (31ft 9in), Height 4.33m (14ft 2in)
**Powerplant:** Two Liming Wopen-6A afterburning turbojets, each rated at 29.42kN (6,610lbf) thrust dry, 36.78kN (8,270lbf) with afterburner
**Maximum speed:** 1210km/h (752mph)
**Range:** 2000km (1200 miles)
**Ceiling:** 16,500m (54,100ft)
**Crew:** 1
**Armament:** Two Norinco Type 23-2K 23mm (0.9in) cannon; up to 2000kg (4400lb) of fuel or ordnance on 10 hardpoints

## ATTACK, BOMBER, & ANTI-SUBMARINE AIRCRAFT

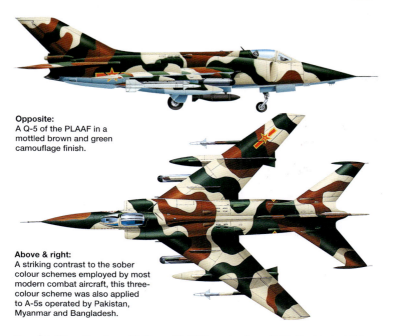

**Opposite:**
A Q-5 of the PLAAF in a mottled brown and green camouflage finish.

**Above & right:**
A striking contrast to the sober colour schemes employed by most modern combat aircraft, this three-colour scheme was also applied to A-5s operated by Pakistan, Myanmar and Bangladesh.

People's Liberation Army Air Force (PLAAF) service from 1962. Designated F-6 for export, the type proved successful, mainly due to its affordability.

### Lingering presence

Retired in the late 1990s in China, a few J-6s linger on in service in foreign nations with North Korea possessing the largest fleet, though it is unknown how many remain serviceable. Further Chinese development saw the appearance of a dedicated ground attack variant, the Q-5 (A-5 when exported) which featured a radically changed appearance due to the jet engine intakes being moved from the extreme nose to the fuselage sides, allowing space in the nose for a radar (though this was never actually fitted). A-5s remain in service today with Sudan and Myanmar, the latter nation using theirs in combat as recently as 2015 in strikes against the Myanmar National Democratic Alliance Army.

ATTACK, BOMBER, & ANTI-SUBMARINE AIRCRAFT

# Soko J-22 Orao

A joint venture between Romania and Yugoslavia, the J-22 was developed in the 1970s as a cost-effective lightweight attack aircraft and remains in service with the Serbian Air Force.

Both Romania and Yugoslavia wished to avoid over-reliance on Soviet-supplied military equipment and in 1970 began collaborating on the design of a comparatively simple attack aircraft to replace the F-84 and Jastreb in Yugoslavia and the MiG-15 and -17 in Romania. Although a supersonic aircraft with a single engine, difficulties obtaining a suitable engine saw the aircraft emerge as a

Serbian Air Force Soko J-22 Orao fighter jet at the Kecsemet Airshow.

### Soko J-22 Orao

**Weight (maximum take-off):** 11,080kg (24,427lb)
**Dimensions:** Length 14.90m (48ft 11in), Wingspan 9.30m (30ft 6in), Height 4.52m (14ft 10in)
**Powerplant:** Two Orao/Turbomecanica built Rolls-Royce Viper Mk 633-47 afterburning turbojets, each rated at 17.79kN (4,000lbf) thrust dry

**Maximum speed:** 1130km/h (700 mph)
**Range:** 1320km (820 miles) ferry range with external fuel
**Ceiling:** 15,000m (49,000ft)
**Crew:** 1
**Armament:** Two fixed 23mm (0.91in) Gryazev-Shipunov GSh-23L twin barrel cannon; up to 2800kg (6200lb) ordnance and fuel

## ATTACK, BOMBER, & ANTI-SUBMARINE AIRCRAFT

**Opposite & right:**
This is the first Yugoslavian prototype Orao which is now preserved in this scheme in the Aviodrome in Belgrade.

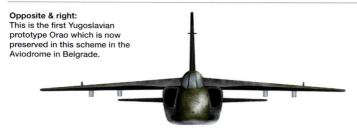

**The two-seat reconnaissance Orao variant is designated the NJ-22. Serbia undertook a major upgrade to its Orao fleet in the late 2010s.**

twin-engine design featuring the Rolls-Royce Viper, which Soko was already building under licence.

### Serbian service

The resulting aircraft was known as the IAR-93 Vultur in Romania and J-22 Orao ('Eagle') in Yugoslavia. For political reasons, prototypes made simultaneous first flights in both nations on 31 October 1974 and the aircraft entered service with Romania in 1975, with Yugoslavia following suit in 1978. The collapse of Yugoslavia into internecine conflict in the 1990s saw the J-22 conduct airstrikes in Croatia in 1991 and the Oraos fell into the hands of several successor states. By 2025 all operational aircraft were serving with the Serbian Air Force and these are expected to continue flying into the 2030s.

ATTACK, BOMBER, & ANTI-SUBMARINE AIRCRAFT

# Sukhoi Su-22 'Fitter'

**Although nearing the end of its career, the Su-22 remains an important part of the Polish Air Force as well as serving with a handful of other nations.**

The Su-22 is a re-engined version of the Su-17, the Soviet Union's first variable geometry aircraft to enter production. The 'swing wing' Su-17 had been developed as a variant of the Su-7 to improve the lengthy take-off and landing run of that aircraft in the wake of a realization that very long concrete runways were attractive, and vulnerable, targets. The Su-17 flew in August 1966 and entered production

**Wings swept forward, this Polish Su-22M-4 climbs away after take-off.**

### Sukhoi Su-22M4

**Weight (maximum take-off):** 19,430kg (42,836lb)
**Dimensions:** Length 19.02m (62ft 5in), Wingspan 13.68m (44ft 11in) wings spread, Height 5.12m (16ft 10in)
**Powerplant:** One Tumansky R-29BSz-300 afterburning turbojet engine, 83.6kN (18,794lbf) thrust dry

**Maximum speed:** 1830km/h (1137mph)
**Range:** 2300km (1329 miles)
**Ceiling:** 15,200m (49,868ft)
**Crew:** 1
**Armament:** Two 30mm (1.18in) Nudelman-Rikhter NR-30 cannon fixed forward firing in wings; up to 4000kg (8800lb) of bombs or stores

ATTACK, BOMBER, & ANTI-SUBMARINE AIRCRAFT

**Opposite:**
Today exhibited in the Central Air Force Museum in Moscow, this Su-17M-4 is a representative of the final production version of the Fitter.

**Above & below:**
The Su-22 has been a cornerstone of Polish aviation forces for decades. Initially flown in camouflage colours similar to the Soviet example pictured opposite, in recent years most Polish Su-22s have been finished in this low-contrast grey scheme. The swept wing feature of the type is obvious here (left).

the following year. The Su-22 featured a Tumansky R29BS-300 engine that offered similar power to the AL-21F of the Su-17M and, despite being larger and less fuel efficient, was much cheaper.

## Long-service bomber

The Su-22 was supplied to most Warsaw Pact nations but Iraq was the largest single non-Warsaw Pact user, though most of their surviving fleet fled to Iran during the Gulf War, where they were eventually refurbished and pressed into service. Thirty Iranian Su-22s are believed to be still operational and these aircraft were upgraded in 2018, reportedly allowing them to carry smart bombs, transfer data from unmanned aerial vehicles (UAVs) and fire air-launched cruise missiles (ALCMs). In early 2025, Poland maintained a fleet of 12 single-seaters and six two-seat Su-22s, the last operational examples in Europe.

ATTACK, BOMBER, & ANTI-SUBMARINE AIRCRAFT

# Sukhoi Su-24 'Fencer'

> One of the most successful Soviet combat aircraft of the 1970s, thanks to a succession of upgrades, the Fencer remains a formidable strike asset.

In the mid 1960s, Sukhoi began work on the aircraft that would become the Su-24, initially pursuing a design with four Kolesov RD-36-35 lift jets in a bay behind the cockpit, arranged near-vertically to provide additional lift and deliver short take-off and landing (STOL) performance. This arrangement was dropped and replaced by a variable geometry wing to deliver adequate take-off and

This Su-24 was displayed during the celebration of the centenary of the Russian Air Force in August 2012 at Zhukovsky.

### Sukhoi Su-24

**Weight (maximum take-off):** 43,755kg (96,463lb)
**Dimensions:** Length 22.53m (73ft 11in), Wingspan 17.64m (57ft 10in) wings spread, Height 6.19m (20ft 4in)
**Powerplant:** Two Lyulka AL-21F-3A afterburning turbojet engines, each rated at 75kN (17,000lbf) thrust dry

**Maximum speed:** 1654km/h (1028mph)
**Range:** 2775km (1724 miles) ferry range with drop tanks
**Ceiling:** 11,000m (36,090ft)
**Crew:** 2
**Armament:** One 23mm (0.91in) Gryazev-Shipunov GSh-6-23M rotary cannon fixed; up to 8000kg (17,635lb) bombs, missiles or stores

## ATTACK, BOMBER, & ANTI-SUBMARINE AIRCRAFT

**Opposite:**
'08 Blue' is a Fencer-D, the Su-24M, which began to enter service in 1986 and is pictured here in Soviet markings.

**Left & below:**
This 'Fencer-C' is from the 4th Squadron of the 234th Air Regiment based in Kubinka and wears an unusual brown and green over blue camouflage scheme, most Russian Su-24s being overall grey.

landing performance while also providing a high cruising speed. The first flight took place on 17 January 1970, and the first production aircraft appeared in December 1971 with the first Soviet Air Force unit forming on the Su-24 in 1973, becoming operational two years later.

### Combat use

Initially subject to an export ban, this restriction was lifted and Syria, Libya, Algeria and Iraq all obtained Su-24s. Iran became a Fencer user after Iraqi Su-24s flew to Iran at the outset of the 1991 Gulf War and subsequently ordered a further 14 examples from Russia. In 2025, Russian Aerospace forces are the largest user and both Russia and Ukraine have utilized the Su-24 during the conflict in Ukraine, both sides suffering losses.

ATTACK, BOMBER, & ANTI-SUBMARINE AIRCRAFT

# Sukhoi Su-25 'Frogfoot'

A heavily armoured ground-attack and close support aircraft, the Su-25 has seen action in several conflicts, most recently on both sides during the Russian invasion of Ukraine.

Developed by the Sukhoi Design Bureau in Moscow, work on what became the Su-25 began in 1968 and the prototype first flew on 22 February 1975. Two test aircraft, the T8-1D and T8-3, were deployed to Afghanistan for trials in 1980 before 12 aircraft were delivered in April 1981. Subsonic but highly manoeuvrable and a delight to fly, the Su-25 was produced in both single- and two-seat variants,

Formation take-off by a single- and two-seater Frogfoot. Excellent handling has seen the Su-25 much used in training roles.

### Sukhoi Su-25TM

**Weight (maximum take-off):** 21,500kg (47,400lb)
**Dimensions:** Length 15.06m (49ft 5in), Wingspan 14.36m (47ft 1in), Height 5.2m (17ft 1in)
**Powerplant:** Two Tumansky R-195 turbojet engines, each rated at 44.18kN (9930lbf)

**Maximum speed:** 950km/h (590mph)
**Range:** 1050km (652 miles)
**Ceiling:** 7000m (22,965ft)
**Crew:** 1
**Armament:** One 30mm (1.18in) Gryazev-Shipunov GSh-30-2 Gast cannon; up to 4400kg (9700lb) bombs, missiles, gun pods or stores

## ATTACK, BOMBER, & ANTI-SUBMARINE AIRCRAFT

**Below:**
The crudely applied Z markings of Russian forces in Ukraine are apparent on this Su-25. By April 2025 Russia had lost 38 Su-25s in Ukraine, more than any other fixed-wing type.

**Opposite:**
As the tensions of the Cold War eased somewhat, this Czechoslovak Su-25 visited Kleine Brogel Air Base's open day in August 1991.

**Above:**
This two-seater Su-25SM was shot down and destroyed by a Ukrainian man-portable air defence system (MANPADS) in March 2022. The pilot managed to eject and return to Russian-held territory.

most of the latter retaining full combat capability and thus able to rapidly switch between training and combat roles. As well as its use in Afghanistan, the Su-25 proved highly effective in the Iran–Iraq War, flying approximately 900 sorties but only losing one aircraft to ground fire.

### Ukraine War service

Following the breakup of the Soviet Union, several successor states inherited Su-25 fleets, many of which remain in service. The largest user, unsurprisingly, is the Russian Aerospace Forces, which had 192 aircraft on strength in 2021, but this number has been reduced by at least 38 due to losses in Ukraine. Russian aircraft received a mid life upgrade in 1999 bringing them up to Su-25SM standard but a second generation Su-25TM (sometimes referred to as the Su-39) has also been produced, though to date in comparatively small numbers.

ATTACK, BOMBER, & ANTI-SUBMARINE AIRCRAFT

# Sukhoi Su-34 'Fullback'

**Derived from the Su-27, the Su-34 is a large strike aircraft intended primarily for tactical interdiction, including attacks on key enemy infrastructure**

In 1986 development of the Su-27IB *Istrebitel-Bombardirovshchik* ('fighter-bomber') was authorized. The new aircraft featured avionics based around the new Sh141 air-to-ground radar system and the first prototype converted from a production Su-27UB flew on 13 April 1990. Compared to the Su-27, the fuselage is modified with a distinctive 'platypus' nose and features canard foreplanes. The pilot

'03 Red' shows off its distinctive 'stinger' between the exhausts in Russia in 2015.

## Sukhoi Su-34

**Weight (maximum take-off):** 45,100kg (99,428lb)
**Dimensions:** Length 24.8m (81ft 4in), Wingspan 14.7m (48ft 3in), Height 6.08m (19ft 11in)
**Powerplant:** Two Saturn AL-31F turbofans, each rated at 122.58kN (27,558lb) thrust with afterburning
**Maximum speed:** Mach 1.6

**Range:** 4000km (2485 miles) ferry range
**Ceiling:** 15,700m (51,509ft)
**Crew:** 2
**Armament:** One GSh-301 30mm (1.18in) cannon; up to 8000kg (17,637lb) of external stores on 12 weapons pylons, including Kh-59M (AS-18 'Kazoo') TV-guided missiles, Kh-31P anti-radar and Kh-31A anti-ship missiles

# ATTACK, BOMBER, & ANTI-SUBMARINE AIRCRAFT

**Opposite:**
This Su-34 was based at Baltimor Air Base near Voronezh, Russia, in 2015. In profile the radically redesigned fuselage, 'duck-billed' nose and massive tail 'sting' are all evident.

**Left & below:**
'42 Blue' was the first flying prototype Su-27IB, which would subsequently be redesignated Su-34.

and navigator/weapons system operator are seated side-by-side in a titanium-alloy armoured 'box', the undercarriage is strengthened to handle the extra weight of the aircraft and features tandem mainwheels, and the tail 'sting' is also considerably enlarged.

## Chechnya and Georgia conflicts

The Su-34 was cleared for initial operational service in October 2006, though test aircraft were involved in the conflicts in Chechnya and Georgia. From September 2015 to late 2024, Su-34s were a regular presence in Syria where they were primarily used to drop unguided ordnance, though they also delivered precision weapons on occasion. Su-34s have been heavily committed to the Russian invasion of Ukraine and a shortage of GPS-guided bomb kits forced the Su-34 crews to fly at low altitude to achieve accurate results and losses have been heavy, with at least 35 shot down, destroyed on the ground or abandoned by mid 2024.

ATTACK, BOMBER, & ANTI-SUBMARINE AIRCRAFT

# Tupolev Tu-95 'Bear'

> As iconic a symbol of the Cold War for the USSR as the B-52 is to the USA, in updated form the Tu-95 remains in operational service with the Russian Aerospace Forces.

Featuring the unusual combination of a swept wing with turboprop propulsion, the Tu-95 was designed to meet a 1951 request to develop an intercontinental bomber with an unrefueled range of 8000km (5000 miles). The Tu-95 prototype flew on 12 November 1952 and production began in 1955, a total of 173 aircraft being built. Intended for the nuclear strike mission, the bomb bay featured

A pair of Tu-95MS 'Bears' display in 2020. The Tu-95 is notable for its extreme longevity.

### Tu-95K

**Weight (maximum take-off):** 188,000kg (414,469lb)
**Dimensions:** Length 46.9m (153ft 3in), Wingspan 50.04m (164ft 2in), Height 12.12m (39ft 9in)
**Powerplant:** Four Kuznetsov 11,190kW (15,000shp) NK-12M turboprop engines
**Maximum speed:** 860km/h (534mph)

**Range:** 12,500km (7770 miles)
**Ceiling:** 11,600m (38,048ft)
**Crew:** 9
**Armament:** Six 23mm (0.91in) Afanasev Makarov AM-23 cannon, mounted in pairs in each of the two remote control turrets and two in manned tail position; up to 10,700kg (23,590lb) bombload

ATTACK, BOMBER, & ANTI-SUBMARINE AIRCRAFT

**Opposite:**
The Tu-95K was designed to carry a Kh-20 cruise missile semi-recessed in its belly. The scanning antenna for the a-336Z guidance radar is housed in the chin radome.

**Above:**
Named 'Veliki Novgorod','16 Red' is one of the Tu-95MS bombers operated by the 184th Heavy Bomber Aviation Regiment at Engels air base.

**Above:**
Tu-95MS '27 Red' is named 'Izborsk' after the eponymous Russian medieval fortress complex. 'Izborsk' is also on the strength of the 184th Heavy Bomber Aviation Regiment.

heating and climate control for the nuclear weapons, which required specific environmental conditions, and the cockpit featured blast visors to protect against the nuclear flash. Alternatively, the Tu-95 could carry up to 20 tonnes of conventional bombs, and in the 1970s, the Tu-95 switched to the role of missile carrier rather than conventional freefall bomber, a role which it continues to perform today.

### Veteran bomber

Despite already serving for nearly 60 years, the Tu-95 was used in active combat service for the first time in 2015 when aircraft delivered missile strikes against targets in Syria. Subsequently, Tu-95s took part in the opening assault of Russia's invasion of Ukraine in February 2022, launching cruise missiles in concert with Tu-160s. Today, the majority of Russia's Tu-95s are of upgraded Tu-95MSM standard with new avionics and systems and modified engine and propellers for improved efficiency.

159

ATTACK, BOMBER, & ANTI-SUBMARINE AIRCRAFT

# Tupolev Tu-22M3 'Backfire'

**For over 40 years, the variable-geometry Tu-22M has served as a supersonic intermediate-range bomber and missile carrier, intended to deliver both nuclear and conventional weapons.**

After the disappointing performance of the original Tu-22 'Blinder', Tupolev was asked to develop the Tu-22M in 1967. Despite keeping the Tu-22 designation, the Tu-22M was a new design and proved to be a huge improvement over its unfortunate predecessor. The prototype made its first flight in 1969 and production aircraft began to be built in 1973 with the definitive Tu-22M3 appearing in

**The imposing form of the Tu-22M3 as photographed at Tambor, Russia, in May 2014.**

### Tu-22M3

**Weight (maximum take-off):** 12,6000kg (27,7782lb)
**Dimensions:** Length 42.46m (139ft 4in), Wingspan 34.28m (112ft 6in) spread and 23.3m (76ft) swept, Height 11.05m (36ft 3in)
**Powerplant:** Two Kuznetsov NK-25 afterburning turbofan engines, each rated at 145kN (33,000lbf) dry

**Maximum speed:** 1997km/h (1241mph)
**Range:** 6800km (4200 miles)
**Ceiling:** 13,300m (43,600ft)
**Crew:** 4
**Armament:** One 23-mm (0.91in) Gryazev-Shipunov GSh-23 cannon flexibly mounted in remotely controlled tail turret; up to 24,000kg (53,000lb) of bombs or missiles

## ATTACK, BOMBER, & ANTI-SUBMARINE AIRCRAFT

**All images:**
This Soviet Tu-22M3 is carrying a Kh-22 anti-shipping missile. The standard Kh-22 carries a 1000kg (2205lb) high explosive warhead whereas Kh-22P/N variants carry a 3.5kT nuclear warhead and have a range of 550km (340 miles) when launched at high altitude.

1977. Five hundred and fourteen aircraft had been constructed when production ceased in 1993, and the aircraft was never exported. During the Cold War the Backfire was intended to undertake anti-shipping strikes against US Navy aircraft carriers and other major warships.

### Combat role

First used in combat in Afghanistan in 1984, the Tu-22M was used to drop freefall bombs, a task it repeated in Chechnya during the mid 1990s and then in Georgia and Syria. Since April 2022 Tu-22M3s have been active in the conflict in Ukraine, launching Kh-22 missiles and dropping unguided bombs on Mariupol. Although several Backfires have been lost during the conflict, none has yet been confirmed destroyed in air combat. The most recent upgrade sees Russian aircraft upgraded to Tu-22M3M status with new radar, navigation system, communication suite, IFF and digital flight control system.

ATTACK, BOMBER, & ANTI-SUBMARINE AIRCRAFT

# Tupolev Tu-142 'Bear'

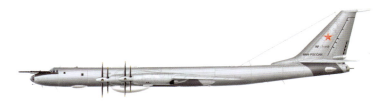

A dedicated long-range ASW version of the 'Bear', the Tu-142 entered service in 1972 and has continued its maritime duties ever since, receiving several upgrades during its operational life.

The first prototype of the Tu-142 flew on 18 July 1968, differing from the Tu-95 most obviously in that its forward fuselage was stretched by 1.7m (5ft 7in), allowing for a larger cockpit to improve crew comfort and providing space for the aircraft's systems. The flight deck was also raised slightly to improve visibility for the flight crew. The Tu-142 also featured an extended chord wing, deleted dorsal and ventral

The Tu-142 can easily be distinguished from the Tu-95 by the MAD boom on the tip of the vertical tail.

### Tupolev Tu-142 'Bear'

**Weight (maximum take-off):** 185,000kg (407,855lb)
**Dimensions:** Length 49.5m (162ft 5in), Wingspan 51.1m (167ft 8in), Height 12.12m (39ft 9in)
**Powerplant:** Four 11,033kW (14,795hp) Kuznetsov NK-12MV turboprop engines
**Maximum speed:** 825km/h (513mph)

**Range:** 12,550km (7800 miles)
**Ceiling:** 13,500m (44,291ft)
**Crew:** 10
**Armament:** Two 23mm (0.91in) Afanasev Makarov AM-23 cannon flexibly mounted in rear turret; up to 11,340kg of missiles, torpedoes, depth charges or stores, typically eight Kh-35 anti-ship missiles

## ATTACK, BOMBER, & ANTI-SUBMARINE AIRCRAFT

**Above & below:**
Tu-142MZ 'Bear-F's such as this one have been considerably more active since 2020 and NATO exercises, such as the nine-nation 'Joint Viking 25' off Tromsø, Norway, have attracted particular attention from Tu-142s.

**Opposite top:**
The Tu-142's main sensor equipment is the Korshun ('Kite') radar which is housed in the large ventral fairing.

turrets and utilized NK-12MV engines, nearly a third more powerful than the NK-12Ms of the Tu-95.

The Berkut ('Golden Eagle') search radar, originally developed for the Ilyushin Il-38, formed the core of the aircraft's combat systems, complemented by electronic intelligence (ELINT), infrared detection and sonobuoy receiver systems. A weapons bay was positioned behind the main radar fairing for carrying depth charges, homing torpedoes, mines or sonobuoys.

### Russian Navy service

Over 100 Tu-142s were completed and currently the Russian Navy maintains two Tu-142 squadrons, for a total of around 16 airworthy aircraft. In addition, the Russian Navy operates around eight Tu-142MR/MRM submarine communications relay aircraft. In addition to the USSR and Russia, the Indian Navy operated eight Tu-142s from 1988 until 2017 when they were retired and replaced by the Boeing P-8I Poseidon.

ATTACK, BOMBER, & ANTI-SUBMARINE AIRCRAFT

# Tupolev Tu-160 'Blackjack'

> One of the last aircraft designs developed in the Soviet Union, the Tu-160 is both the largest supersonic combat aircraft ever built and the largest swing-wing aircraft ever built.

The Tu-160 began life with a 1967 requirement for a long-range supersonic strategic bomber which by the early 1970s was best met by Myasishchev's 'swing wing' M-20 design. However, this project was passed to Tupolev due to that design bureau's familiarity with large variable geometry aircraft.

Development of such a complicated aircraft took time and

With wings at medium sweep, a Tu-160 displays at a 2015 air show in Samara.

### Tu-160

**Weight (maximum take-off):** 275,000kg (606,271lb)
**Dimensions:** Length 54.1m (177ft 6in), Wingspan 55.7m (182ft 9in) wings spread, 35.6m (116ft 10in) wings swept, Height 13.1m (43ft)
**Powerplant:** Four Kuznetsov NK-32 afterburning turbofan engines, each rated at 137.3kN (30,900lbf) dry, 245kN (55,000lbf) with afterburner
**Maximum speed:** 2220km/h (1380mph)
**Range:** 12,300km (7600 miles)
**Ceiling:** 16,000m (52,000ft)
**Crew:** 4
**Armament:** Up to 45,000kg (99,208lb) of bombs or missiles

## ATTACK, BOMBER, & ANTI-SUBMARINE AIRCRAFT

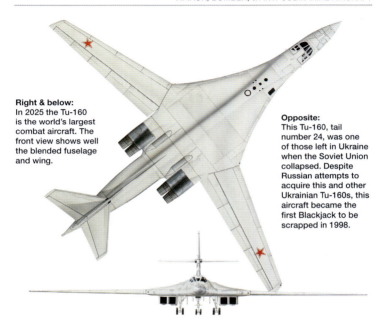

**Right & below:**
In 2025 the Tu-160 is the world's largest combat aircraft. The front view shows well the blended fuselage and wing.

**Opposite:**
This Tu-160, tail number 24, was one of those left in Ukraine when the Soviet Union collapsed. Despite Russian attempts to acquire this and other Ukrainian Tu-160s, this aircraft became the first Blackjack to be scrapped in 1998.

although the first prototype flew in December 1981 it would be 1984 before the second prototype appeared. The Tu-160 became operational in April 1987 and initially operated primarily as a cruise missile carrier carrying six Kh-55 long-range weapons or up to 12 Kh-15 short-range nuclear missiles, though conventional freefall bombs could be carried. Thirty-two operational Tu-160s had been built, with four more in assembly (all of which were eventually completed, the last as late as 2018) when the Soviet Union collapsed.

### Restarting production

However, Russian production restarted in 2022 and 50 new-build aircraft were on order in 2024. The Tu-160 was used in action for the first time during strikes in Syria in 2015 utilizing Kh-101 cruise missiles air-launched over the Mediterranean. More recently, sporadic Tu-160 missions to launch cruise missiles have been flown against Ukraine since 2022.

ATTACK, BOMBER, & ANTI-SUBMARINE AIRCRAFT

# Xi'an H-6 'Badger'

A basic design of astonishing longevity, the H-6 is the Chinese version of the Tupolev Tu-16 which remained in production in 2025 despite the Tu-16 first flying in 1952.

Arrangements were undertaken for licence production of the Tu-16 to go ahead in China in the mid 1950s. The first completely domestically produced Tu-16 appeared in 1969, though aircraft had been assembled in China from Russian-supplied parts since 1959, and the H-6 was initially intended to operate as a nuclear bomber. During the 1970s, a shift in role saw the H-6 increasingly used as

An H-6K lands at Dyagilevo Air Base in Russia during the 2018 Aviadarts international flight skills competition.

### Xi'an H-6K

**Weight (maximum take-off):** 95,000kg (209,439lb)
**Dimensions:** Length 34.8m (114ft 2in), Wingspan 33m (108ft 3in), Height 10.36m (34ft)
**Powerplant:** Two Soloviev D-30KP-2 turbofan engines each rated at 118kN (27,000lb) thrust

**Maximum speed:** 1050km/h (650mph)
**Range:** 3500km (2200 miles)
**Ceiling:** 12,800m (42,000ft)
**Crew:** 4
**Armament:** Six underwing pylons for air-launched KD-20 or KD-63 land-attack cruise missiles

## ATTACK, BOMBER, & ANTI-SUBMARINE AIRCRAFT

**Opposite:**
This H-6K is operated by the PLAAF's 108th Air Regiment which has operated successive variants of the H-6 since the mid 1960s and currently flies both the H-6K and the H-6M from Wugong, Shaanxi Province.

**Below:**
The H-6N carries an air-launched anti-ship ballistic missile, probably a variant of the DF-21 anti-ship missile.

**Right:** Proof that although it remains in production, the H-6 is a literal museum piece: one of the PLAAF's original H-6 bombers on display in the central exhibition hall of the Military Museum, Beijing.

a missile carrier. The H-6K featuring a new nose incorporating a large radome appeared in 2006, again intended as a cruise missile carrier, with up to six missiles carried under the wings. The H-6K also features enlarged air intakes for its Soloviev turbofans, replacing the WP-8 turbojets of earlier versions.

## Long-range version

A longer-range version for the navy was also produced as the H-6J as well as the H-6N dedicated to enormous anti-ship ballistic missiles, only one of which may be carried. A separate line of development has seen the H-6 design reworked into an airborne tanker, produced for both air force and naval use. Two hundred and thirty-one H-6s had been built by 2020 and production continues at the Xi'an factory at the time of writing.

ATTACK, BOMBER, & ANTI-SUBMARINE AIRCRAFT

# Xi'an JH-7 'Flounder'

A supersonic twin-engine tactical strike and maritime attack aircraft, the JH-7 was developed in the 1970s but its development was extremely prolonged and it entered service only in the 1990s.

Development of the JH-7 began as a result of the 1974 Battle of the Paracel Islands, when the naval forces of China engaged those of South Vietnam and the Chinese discovered that they had a serious deficiency in air support capability. Proposals for a strike aircraft were sought in 1975 but producing a common airframe for both air force and navy proved difficult due to the differing requirements of both

A JH-7 taxies in at Dyagilevo Air Base in Russia during the Avidarts 2018 competition.

### Xi'an JH-7A

**Weight (maximum take-off):** 28,475kg (62,777lb)
**Dimensions:** Length 22.32m (73ft 3in), Wingspan 12.8m (42ft), Height 6.22m (20ft 5in)
**Powerplant:** Two WS-9 turbofan engines each rated at 91.26kN (20,520lb) thrust with afterburning
**Maximum speed:** Mach 1.52

**Range:** Around 1760km (1090 miles) with one inflight refuelling
**Ceiling:** 16,000m (52,000ft)
**Crew:** 2
**Armament:** One 23mm (0.9in) twin-barrel GSh-23 cannon plus a maximum of 9000kg (20,000lb) of disposable stores carried on nine hardpoints

## ATTACK, BOMBER, & ANTI-SUBMARINE AIRCRAFT

**Opposite:**
Serving with the PLAAF's 126th Air Brigade, part of the Nanning Base, within Southern Theatre Command, this JH-7A is stationed at Liuzhou, China.

**Above & right:**
The marked anhedral of the JH-7A is evident when viewed from the front. The JH-7A has a lighter and stronger airframe than the JH-7, allowing the newer aircraft to carry a maximum ordnance load of 9000kg (20,000lbs).

services. No engine of sufficient power was available either and so when the design was finalized in 1983, the British Rolls-Royce Spey was selected, initially imported but to be replaced with Chinese licence-built Speys, designated WS-9, when they became available.

## Service

The aircraft finally flew in 1988 but by this time the air force had decided to acquire the Su-30MKK. The navy pressed on with the JH-7 programme, however, and the aircraft officially entered service in 1994. The domestically produced WS-9 engine was integrated in 2007. Air force interest was reawakened by the JH-7's low cost and long range by which time development of the improved JH-7A had been undertaken and both air force and navy units introduced this variant in 2004.

# Transport & Reconnaissance

Armies need to be moved to combat theatres and commanders need to know what the enemy is up to. All major air arms possess transport aircraft in a variety of sizes to suit various operational needs to deliver troops and supplies, while the task of reconnoitering fixed positions, troop movements, armour build ups and so on initially gave rise to military aircraft in the first place. The sophistication of the sensory equipment carried aloft by modern reconnaissance aircraft is, however, an order of magnitude beyond anything that has come before.

**Opposite: An Airbus A400M Atlas four-engined military transport aircraft stands on the runway at RAF Fairford, UK.**

TRANSPORT AND RECONNAISSANCE

# Airbus A400M Atlas

Intended as a replacement for the C-130 Hercules C-160 Transall C-160 in several air arms, over 120 examples of the multinational A400M have been constructed to date.

Despite a painfully slow development (the origins of the A400 programme can be traced back to 1982), spiralling costs and a fatal crash in 2015, the Airbus A400M is now serving with nine air forces and is on order with a tenth.

Offering a greater cargo capacity than the C-130 Hercules but with better rough-field performance than the C-17 Globemaster, the Atlas

The Airbus A400M prototype makes its international air show debut at Farnborough, United Kingdom, in 2010.

### Airbus A400M Atlas

**Weight (maximum take-off):** 141,000kg (310,852lb)
**Dimensions:** Length 45.1m (148ft 0in), Wingspan 42.4m (139ft 1in), Height 14.7m (48ft 3in)
**Powerplant:** Four 8200kW (11,000hp) Europrop TP400-D6 turboprops

**Maximum speed:** 750kmh (466mph)
**Range:** 6400km (3977 miles) with 20 tonne payload
**Ceiling:** 12,200m (40,000ft)
**Crew:** 3–4
**Maximum payload:** 37,000kg (81,600lb)

TRANSPORT AND RECONNAISSANCE

**Opposite:**
The RAF operates 22 A400Ms which it designates the Atlas C.1. RAF Atlas aircraft regularly conduct training on Pembrey Beach in west Wales to practice operating from unprepared natural surfaces.

**Above:**
A Belgian Air Force A400M of the 15th Air Transport Wing (known in Dutch as 15 Wing Luchttransport, and French as 15 Wing Transport Aérien). Belgium maintains a fleet of seven A400Ms.

**Above:**
France was the first nation to receive a production A400M and the first to use the A400M operationally; on 29 December 2013, a French aircraft supported Operation Serval in Mali.

usefully occupies a niche position, straddling tactical and strategic transport requirements.

## Agile lifter

Although a generally conventional military airlifter, the A400M is notably agile for an aircraft of its size and features a somewhat unusual engine arrangement with two of its eight-bladed propellers rotating clockwise and the other two counterclockwise (two of each on each wing), a feature that improves lift and handling, especially in the event of engine failure. Its Europrop TP400-D6 engines, developed specifically to power this aircraft, are the most powerful turboprops to enter production in Western Europe to date. Like most contemporary aircraft, it features a 'glass cockpit' with digital avionics.

TRANSPORT AND RECONNAISSANCE

# Airbus C-295

A versatile tactical transport, the C-295 has been employed for medical evacuation, electronic intelligence (ELINT) and maritime patrol use. Armed variants exist for special operations work.

CASA developed the CN-235 jointly with IPTN of Indonesia in the early 1980s as a larger transport aircraft to complement the highly successful C-212. First flown in November 1983, the CN-235 was primarily intended for military use and features a tail ramp for simple loading and unloading as well as short take-off and landing (STOL) capability, and proved popular. The latest iteration of

EC-296 was the second prototype of the C-295, appearing in 1998, and continues to perform development work today. The prominent winglets were added in 2014.

## Airbus C-295

**Weight (maximum take-off):** 23,200kg (51,147lb)
**Dimensions:** Length 24.50m (80ft), Wingspan 27.59m (91ft), Height 8.66m (28ft)
**Powerplant:** Two 1,972kW (2644hp) Pratt & Whitney Canada PW127G turboprops

**Maximum speed:** 550km/h (342mph)
**Range:** 5000km (3107 miles) with 3000kg (6614lb) payload
**Ceiling:** 7620m (25,000ft)
**Crew:** 2
**Maximum payload:** 9000kg (19,842lb)

# TRANSPORT AND RECONNAISSANCE

**Opposite:**
The Mexican Navy operates four C-295Ms and two C-295Ws, as pictured above. The Naval C-295 fleet is based at the Tapachula Air Naval Base, near the border of Mexico and Guatemala.

**Below:**
A Polish Air Force C-295M lands at Zeltweg Air Base in Austria in 2019. Poland was the first export customer for the C-295, ordering it in 2001.

**The Vietnamese People's Air Force operates three Airbus C-295s for the airlift, medical evacuation and logistical transport roles.**

the CN-235 airframe is the Airbus C-295 (CASA was absorbed into the Airbus group in 2000) that entered service in 2001.

## Export success

Effectively a stretched CN-235, the C-295 can carry up to 48 paratroops and features more powerful engines for improved speed, range and payload. As a useful upgrade of a familiar type the C-295 has proved highly successful and has been acquired by 36 air arms worldwide. A light gunship version of both types has been developed and Turkish company Roketsan has produced the C-295W for armed special-operations support with their laser-guided 70mm (2.75in) rockets, UMTAS anti-armour missiles and the Teber precision-guidance system for standard bombs.

TRANSPORT AND RECONNAISSANCE

# Airbus MRTT

Airbus has developed two forms of multirole tanker transport (MRTT), one converted from the A310 airliner and a new-build version based on the larger A330 airframe.

The MRTT concept allows for the aircraft to be utilized as a conventional transport when it is not operating in the airborne tanker role, greatly increasing its versatility and cost-effectiveness. Airbus markets the aircraft as a replacement for the Boeing 707-derived KC-135 as that aircraft reaches retirement age. Germany and Canada employ a version of the A310 airliner converted

The A330 MRTT is the longest aircraft ever to be operated by the RAF. This example appeared at the 2018 Royal International Air Tattoo.

### Airbus A330 MRTT

**Weight (maximum take-off):** 233,000kg (514,000lb)
**Dimensions:** Length 58.80m (193ft), Wingspan 60.3m (198ft), Height 17.4m (57ft)
**Powerplant:** Two Rolls-Royce Trent 772B, General Electric CF6-80E1A4 or Pratt & Whitney PW 4170 turbofans, each rated at 320kN (72,000lbf)

**Maximum speed:** 880km/h (547mph)
**Range:** 1800km (1118 miles) with 50 tonnes of fuel
**Ceiling:** 13,000m (42,700ft)
**Crew:** 3
**Payload:** 111,000kg (245,000lb) of fuel or 45,000kg (99,000lb) payload

# TRANSPORT AND RECONNAISSANCE

**Opposite & below:**
In RAAF service the MRTT is designated the KC-30A and operated by No. 33 Squadron based at RAAF Base Amberley near Brisbane in Queensland.

**The Armee de l'Air ordered 15 A330 MRTTs and named them the Phénix. This example was caught departing Luqa airport in Malta in June 2023.**

from aircraft that were already in service with the air arms of those nations as transport aircraft.

## A330 MRTT

But as of 2025, Airbus has also produced 61 examples of the larger, purpose-built A330 MRTT which serve with 11 air forces worldwide including Australia, Canada, France and the UK, and the aircraft remains in serial production. In addition, the aircraft initially won a competition to replace the KC-135 in US Air Force (USAF) service but this award was subsequently (and controversially) cancelled following protests from Boeing and no examples of the KC-45, as it was to be designated, were ever built.

TRANSPORT AND RECONNAISSANCE

# Antonov An-12 'Cub'

> The Soviet Union's equivalent of the C-130 Hercules, the An-12 has proved similarly successful with hundreds remaining in service with dozens of civil and military operators worldwide.

A four-engined development of Antonov's earlier An-8 'Camp', the An-12 has conclusively eclipsed its twin-engine progenitor, having served with over 30 air forces. Initially flown in 1957, the aircraft entered service with the USSR two years later and remains an active component of the Russian transport fleet today, both with Aerospace Forces and Russian Naval Aviation,

The An-12 is a notoriously smoky aircraft as ably displayed by this Russian Air Force An-12BK.

### Antonov An-12

**Weight (maximum take-off):** 61,000kg (134,482lb)
**Dimensions:** Length 33.1m (108ft 7in), Wingspan 38m (124ft 8in), Height 10.53m (34ft 7in)
**Powerplant:** Four 3125kW (4250hp) Ivchenko AI-20K turboprop engines
**Maximum speed:** 777km/h (483mph)

**Range:** 5700km (3500 miles)
**Ceiling:** 10,200m (33,500ft)
**Crew:** 5
**Armament:** Two 23mm (0.91in) Nudelman-Rikhter NR-23 cannon flexibly mounted in rear turret
**Maximum payload:** 20,000kg (44,000lb)

TRANSPORT AND RECONNAISSANCE

**Opposite:**
Initially, An-12s were operated in a natural metal scheme as seen here on '35 Blue'.

**Above (both images):**
This Russian Air Force An-12BK, '25 Blue', was built in 1970 and remains in service in 2025, though the rear armament is no longer fitted to the aircraft and the gunner's glazing has been faired over. Like many Soviet transports, the An-12 possessed quite a potent defensive armament in the form of two 23mm (0.91in) cannon.

as well as continuing to serve in the air forces of a few other nations and in the hands of many civil operators.

## Tactical role

In contrast to the C-130, the An-12 does not feature a pressurized cargo bay (though some later Chinese variants have gained this feature) and is therefore restricted to the tactical role. As originally designed, the An-12 also featured a potent defensive armament with a manned twin 23mm (0.91in) gun position mounted at the tail, though over the course of its service life the vast majority of An-12s had these weapons removed.

TRANSPORT AND RECONNAISSANCE

# Antonov An-26 'Curl'

> A useful tactical transport of medium size, the An-26 remains an important aircraft in many air forces, particularly those of ex Warsaw Pact nations.

Introduced to service in 1970 and given the NATO reporting name 'Curl', the An-26 is an improved development of the earlier An-24 tactical transport, itself still in service in considerable numbers around the world. The main difference between the two aircraft is the addition of a rear loading ramp, allowing the An-26 to be used by paratroops and for air dropping cargo as well as

This Meridian Antonov An-26-100 was photographed landing in Malta in 2015.

### Antonov An-26

**Weight (maximum take-off):** 24,000kg (52,911lb)
**Dimensions:** Length 23.8m (78ft 1in), Wingspan 29.3m (96ft 2in), Height 8.58m (28ft 2in)
**Powerplant:** Two 2103kW (2820hp) Progress AI-24VT Turboprop engines and one 7.85kN (1760lbf) Tumansky turbojet booster rated at 7.85kN (1760lbf)
**Maximum speed:** 540km/h (340mph)
**Range:** 2500km (1600 miles)
**Ceiling:** 7500m (24,600ft)
**Crew:** 6
**Maximum payload:** 5500kg (12,125lb)

TRANSPORT AND RECONNAISSANCE

**Opposite:**
China operates 27 examples of the Xi'an Y-7 including this Y-7H, an unauthorized An-26 copy.

**Above:**
Pictured as it appeared in September 2022, '27 Red' features a tally of mission markings behind the cockpit glazing, presumably representing active operations in Ukraine.

**Above:**
This Russian Naval An-26, '30 Blue' was built in 1979 and wears a distinctive killer whale artwork just behind the cockpit glazing.

permitting simple loading and unloading of vehicles. A unique feature of the An-26's ramp design is that it can be retracted below the fuselage, allowing a truck to back right up to the rear fuselage of the aircraft.

## Export success

Today, the largest military operator of the An-26 is Russia, with around 100 in service in 2025, and there are small numbers serving with around 20 other air arms worldwide. Like many Soviet designs, both the An-24 and An-26 have been manufactured in China, as the Xi'an Y-7 and Y-7H respectively, and both types remain in service with the People's Liberation Army Air Force (PLAAF).

TRANSPORT AND RECONNAISSANCE

# Antonov An-124 Ruslan 'Condor'

**Although more widely employed by civil operators, the massive An-124 is the largest aircraft flown by the Russian Aerospace Forces, its only military operator.**

Developed during the 1970s, the An-124 made its maiden flight in 1982 and entered Soviet service in 1986. Though shorter than the American C-5 Galaxy which it broadly resembles, the An-124 possesses a greater wingspan and is capable of carrying a heavier payload. Cargo may be loaded by the front or rear doors and the undercarriage can lower or 'kneel' to assist loading or unloading.

By 2025, most active An-124s were flying in civil hands. This Antonov Airlines An-124 was pictured taking off from Kabul in 2004.

### Antonov An-124 Ruslan

**Weight (maximum take-off):** 402,000kg (886,258lb)
**Dimensions:** Length 69.1m (226ft 8in), Wingspan 73.3m (240ft 6in), Height 21.08m (69ft 2in)
**Powerplant:** Four Progress D-18T turbofan engines, each rated at 229kN (51000lbf)

**Maximum speed:** 865km/h (537mph)
**Range:** 14,000km (8700 miles)
**Ceiling:** 12,000m (39,000ft)
**Crew:** 6–7
**Maximum payload:** 150,000kg (330,693lb)

## TRANSPORT AND RECONNAISSANCE

**Opposite:**
Russia struggled to keep many of its An-124 fleet operational. RF-82041 had been grounded since 1993 until it was returned to flying status in November 2014.

**Above:**
'10 Black' was one of the first An-124s to be demonstrated in the west and was one of two Soviet examples that visited Farnborough Airshow, UK, in 1990.

**Above:**
Bearing the badge of the 224th Flight Unit, a Russian state-owned cargo operation which was flying six Condors in 2025.

## Production halted

Fifty-four aircraft were built in total. Although plans to restart production of an improved variant of this highly capable aircraft have been proposed since 2010, no An-124s have been manufactured since 2004 due to the economic conditions and the poor diplomatic relations between Russia and Ukraine. Nonetheless, in the absence of new-build aircraft, Russia has undertaken a programme of returning non-airworthy aircraft to service in upgraded An-124-100 form. The first aircraft to be upgraded returned to flight in 2010, over 10 years after it had been grounded.

TRANSPORT AND RECONNAISSANCE

# Beriev A-50 'Mainstay' and KJ-2000 'Mainring'

Both Russia and China's airborne early warning and control (AEW&C) aircraft utilize modified Il-76 airframes equipped with a strut-mounted rotodome to provide 360° radar coverage.

Development of an AEW&C aircraft of similar layout and capability to the US E-3 Sentry took place in the USSR during the late 1960s and 1970s.

The Soviet government ordered the Beriev design bureau to integrate the Shmel ('bumblebee') radar system into an Ilyushin Il-76MD airframe and as such the resultant aircraft became the Beriev

'47 Red' of the Russian Aerospace Forces was the first to be upgraded to A-50U standard with modern electronics and increased crew comfort.

### Beriev A-50

**Weight (maximum take-off):** 170,000kg (374,786lb)
**Dimensions:** Length 49.59m (162ft 8in), Wingspan 50.5m (165ft 8in), Height 14.76m (48ft 5in)
**Powerplant:** Four Soloviev D-30KP turbofan engines, each rated at 117.7kN (26,500lbf)

**Maximum speed:** 900km/h (560mph)
**Range:** 7500km (4700 miles)
**Ceiling:** 12,000m (39,000ft)
**Crew:** 15
**Armament:** N/A

# TRANSPORT AND RECONNAISSANCE

**Opposite:**
'46 Red' is shown in the current standard Russian finish. The A-50 fleet has been utilized in operations over Ukraine and two Mainstays have been shot down since the invasion began.

**Above:**
The Chinese KJ-2000 features a domestically designed and produced phased array radar and associated electronics. The PLAAF operates four such aircraft.

**Above:**
By 2024 Russia was believed to retain just six operational A-50s in service, one of them being A-50U '50 Red'.

A-50. The A-50 entered service in 1984 and has been subject to various upgrades to both airframe and systems.

## Current service

Today, nine aircraft are believed to be operational with Russian Aerospace Forces and the aircraft is also in service with India. An upgraded variant based on the later Il-76MD-90A airframe and with new Premier radar was flown in 2017 as the A-100 but is yet to enter service. In China, the KJ-2000, again based on the Il-76 airframe, features the indigenous Type 88 radar system but problems with Russian Il-76 supply has led China to develop the KJ-3000, flown during 2024, based on the domestically produced Y-20 airframe.

TRANSPORT AND RECONNAISSANCE

# Boeing C-17 Globemaster III

> A large, versatile and exceptionally capable airlifter, the C-17 was in production from 1991 to 2015 and continues to form the backbone of the US transport fleet.

Replacing the C-141 Starlifter in US Air Force (USAF) service, the C-17 features a significantly larger cargo compartment and as such is able to handle loads that were previously only transportable by the C-5 Galaxy. First flown in 1991, the C-17 entered USAF service two years later and with 222 aircraft in service in 2025 is numerically second only to the C-130 Hercules in the US transport inventory.

**Pictured during Operation Enduring Freedom, a USAF C-17 taxies in typically dusty conditions at Bagram Air Base.**

### Boeing C-17A

**Weight (maximum take-off):** 265,352kg (585,000lb)
**Dimensions:** Length 53.04m (174ft), Wingspan 51.77m (169ft 10in), Height 16.79m (55ft 1in)
**Powerplant:** Four Pratt & Whitney F117-PW-100 turbofans, each rated at 179.9kN (40,440lbf)

**Maximum speed:** 829km/h (515mph)
**Range:** 4480km (2780 miles) with 71,214kg (157,000lb) payload
**Ceiling:** 14,000m (45,000ft)
**Crew:** 3
**Maximum payload:** 77,519kg (170,900lb)

TRANSPORT AND RECONNAISSANCE

**Opposite:**
Canada had for several years relied on leased aircraft for its strategic airlift requirements but acquired five C-17s for the RCAF, the last being delivered in 2015.

**Left & below:**
This C-17A was the first production aircraft and was used for testing at Edwards Air Force Base. The Globemaster is equipped with two three-wheel bogies on each side designed to cope with high sink rates and unprepared landing areas. It also features 2.9m (9.5ft) composite winglets that improve aerodynamic efficiency and increase the aircraft's range.

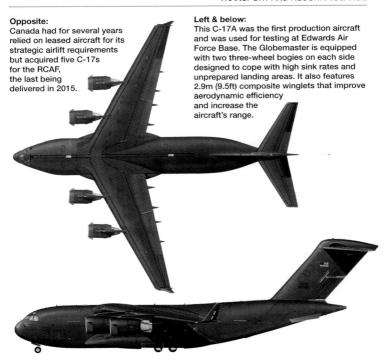

In addition, C-17s serve with the air forces of seven other nations as well as with the multinational Strategic Airlift Capability unit based in Hungary.

## Extensive service

Since the C-17's introduction in the mid 1990s, the aircraft has been heavily committed as both a tactical and strategic transport, a particularly dramatic operation being the night-time airdrop of 1000 paratroopers from 15 C-17s over Bashur, Iraq, in March 2003, the largest combat airdrop since the US invaded Panama in 1989. In addition to its military use, a C-17 accompanies the US president on all overseas trips, carrying the presidential limousine and helicopter.

TRANSPORT AND RECONNAISSANCE

# Boeing E-3 Sentry

> Performing the AWACS (airborne warning and control system) function, and commonly referred to by that acronym, the Boeing E-3 is expected to continue in service until 2035.

The E-3 was developed to replace the piston-engined EC-121 Warning Star, a variant of the 1950s Lockheed Super Constellation airliner that had been in service for over 20 years by the time the Sentry was first delivered to the US Air Force (USAF) in 1977. The E-3 also used an airliner, the Boeing 707, as the basis of its design, onto which is mounted the rotating rotodome housing a Westinghouse-developed

**A USAF Boeing E-3 Sentry arrives prior to the 'Thunder Over the Bay' Air Show at Travis Air Force Base, California, on 28 March 2019.**

### Boeing E-3 Sentry

**Weight (maximum take-off):** 157,397kg (347,000lb)
**Dimensions:** Length 46.61m (152ft 11in), Wingspan 44.42m (145ft 9in), Height 12.60m (41ft 4in)
**Powerplant:** Four Pratt and Whitney TF33-PW-100A turbofans, each rated at 96kN (21,500lbf) thrust

**Maximum speed:** 854km/h (531mph)
**Range:** 7400km (4600 miles)
**Ceiling:** 8800m (29,000ft)
**Crew:** Flight crew 4, mission crew 13–19
**Avionics:** Detection range against medium sized aircraft: approximately 400km (250 miles) for low-flying targets or 650km (400 miles) for medium- to high-altitude targets

# TRANSPORT AND RECONNAISSANCE

**Opposite:** Following the cancellation of the troubled Nimrod AEW.3, the UK relied on the E-3 for its AEW&C requirements from 1991 until 2021 when it was replaced by the E-7 Wedgetail.

**Left & below:** The RAF's E-3 fleet was operated by two units: No. 23 Squadron and No. 8 Squadron, which utilized this aircraft. The squadron's colours can be seen painted on either side of the fuselage roundel.

AN/APY-1 or -2 radar. In 2025 the USAF retained 30 E-3s in service; France and Saudi Arabia operate four and five aircraft respectively. The Royal Air Force (RAF) withdrew its last Sentry in 2021, selling three aircraft to Chile.

## Current service

Unusually, the E-3 is also operated by a joint NATO unit with 14 examples, out of an original inventory of 18, based in Germany. These are manned by 20 multinational crews drawn from 15 member nations with the aircraft nominally registered in Luxembourg.

TRANSPORT AND RECONNAISSANCE

# Boeing E-7 Wedgetail

> Developed to an Australian specification, the E-7 has subsequently been selected by other air forces, including the US Air Force (USAF), as a replacement for the E-3 Sentry.

Named after Australia's largest indigenous eagle, Project Wedgetail was initiated in 1996 to acquire a modern airborne early warning (AEW) platform for the Royal Australian Air Force (RAAF) and in 1999 Boeing was awarded a contract to supply four such aircraft, derived from their ubiquitous 737 airliner. The E-7 features a prominent fixed fairing, known as the 'top hat', on the rear

An RAAF E-7A Wedgetail takes off for a Weapons School Integration mission at Nellis Air Force Base in 2024.

### Boeing E-7 Wedgetail

**Weight (maximum take-off):** 77,600kg (171,000lb)
**Dimensions:** Length 33.6m (110ft 4in), Wingspan 35.8m (117ft 2in), Height 12.5m (41ft 2in)
**Powerplant:** Two CFM International CFM56-7B27A turbofan engines, rated at 12,338kg (27,300lb) thrust each

**Maximum speed:** 870kmh (540mph)
**Range:** 6500km (4000 miles)
**Ceiling:** 12,500m (41,000ft)
**Crew:** 8–10
**Armament:** None

TRANSPORT AND RECONNAISSANCE

**Opposite:**
The RAAF took delivery of its first Wedgetail in 2009 and the aircraft achieved initial operational capability in November 2012. The aircraft are operated by No. 2 Squadron at RAAF Base Williamtown.

**Above:**
The first unit of the RAF to operate the E-7 is No.8 Squadron based at Lossiemouth in Scotland.

**An RAAF E-7A departs after receiving fuel from a KC-135 Stratotanker in support of Operation Inherent Resolve, the campaign against ISIL, in July 2017.**

fuselage containing the Northrop Grumman Electronic Systems Multi-Role Electronically Scanned Array (MESA) radar, which is capable of simultaneous air and sea search, fighter control and area search, with a maximum range of over 600km (370 miles).

### Radar

Despite being fixed, the radar provides a 360° azimuth scan using two electronic arrays on each side, covering two 120° sectors respectively, and a third array housed in the top hat that covers 60° front and aft of the aircraft. Deliveries to Australia began in late 2009 and since then the Wedgetail, also marketed as the Boeing 737 AEW&C, has been ordered by South Korea, Turkey, the UK and US.

TRANSPORT AND RECONNAISSANCE

# Boeing KC-135 Stratotanker & RC-135 Rivet Joint

> Derived from the world's first truly successful jet airliner, the Boeing 707, the C-135 in Stratotanker and Rivet Joint form continues to serve in large numbers with several nations.

The first military development of the 707 was the C-135 Stratolifter, a transport aircraft that entered service in 1961 as a stop gap pending the arrival of the C-141 Starlifter into the US Air Force (USAF) inventory. Variants of the original C-135 were used for a variety of specialist tasks such as weather reconnaissance, trials work and VIP transport but it was as an airborne tanker that the aircraft

Japan-based USAF F-15C Eagles are refuelled by a KC-135 Stratotanker from the 909th Air Refueling Squadron, 2010.

### Boeing KC-135R Stratotanker

**Weight (maximum take-off):** 146,284kg (322,500lb)
**Dimensions:** Length 41.53m (136ft 3in), Wingspan 39.88m (130ft 10in), Height 12.70m (41ft 8in)
**Powerplant:** Four CFM International F108-CF-100 turbofan engines, each rated at 96.2kN (21,600lbf) thrust each

**Maximum speed:** 933km/h (580mph)
**Range:** 2400km (1500 miles)
**Ceiling:** 15,000m (50,000ft)
**Crew:** 3
**Maximum payload:** 90,718kg (200,000lb) of fuel or up to 80 passengers or 38,000kg (83,000lb)

TRANSPORT AND RECONNAISSANCE

**Opposite:**
The 160th Air Refueling Group became the first Air National Guard unit to convert to the KC-135 in 1974. It continued to operate the aircraft until its deactivation in 1993.

**Below:**
Over 60 years after its delivery to the USAF, this RC-135V was on the strength of the 343rd Reconnaissance Squadron in 2025.

An RC-135 Stratoliner aircraft from the 9th Strategic Reconnaissance Wing approaches a KC-135 Stratotanker from the 1700th Air Refueling Squadron Provisional during Operation Desert Shield in 1990.

proved to be particularly useful in USAF service. As the KC-135 Stratotanker, the aircraft proved hugely successful and 803 were built. Despite the last aircraft rolling off the line in 1965, the KC-135 remains in widespread service with 376 in the active USAF inventory at the start of 2025.

## RC-135 Rivet Joint

In the early 1960s the RC-135 appeared for the ELINT and SIGINT (electronic and signals intelligence) role carrying a wide array of surveillance and monitoring equipment which has been augmented, updated and replaced many times over the aircraft's service life. The most significant version in current service is the RC-135V/W Rivet Joint; the USAF has 15 and the Royal Air Force (RAF) three.

TRANSPORT AND RECONNAISSANCE

# Boeing KC-767 & KC-46 Pegasus

> Through a complicated and controversial process, Boeing's 767-derived KC-46 tanker was eventually selected to replace the oldest KC-135s in the US Air Force (USAF) inventory.

The USAF's requirement for a new airborne tanker had become pressing by the early 2000s and Boeing proposed a tanker variant of its 767 airliner to fit the criteria. Ultimately, this aircraft never entered US service after serious corruption came to light leading to the conviction and jailing of several Boeing staff members and the rival Airbus MRTT was selected for the USAF in 2007.

A KC-46 Pegasus is de-iced before take-off in January 2024 at Pease Air National Guard Base, New Hampshire, USA.

### Boeing KC-46 Pegasus

**Weight (maximum take-off):** 188,240kg (415,000lb)
**Dimensions:** Length 50.5m (165ft 6in), Wingspan 48.1m (157ft 8in), Height 15.9m (52ft 1in)
**Powerplant:** Two Pratt & Whitney PW4062 turbofans, each rated at 280kN (62,000lbf) thrust

**Maximum speed:** 914km/h (570mph)
**Range:** 11,830km (7350 miles)
**Ceiling:** 12,200m (40,100ft)
**Crew:** 3 typical, up to 15 additional crew such as medics
**Maximum capacity:** 94,198kg (207,672lb) of fuel or up to 114 passengers, and 29,500kg (65,000lb) payload

TRANSPORT AND RECONNAISSANCE

**Opposite:**
Colombia took delivery of its sole KC-767, which is also used as a VIP transport, in late 2010. The aircraft was converted from a 767 airliner by Israel Aircraft Industries and is named 'Jupiter'.

**Below:**
A typical KC-46A Pegasus of the USAF. Tail number 76033 was delivered in March 2019.

A JASDF KC-767J with its refuelling boom extended. Japan has an inventory of four such aircraft, in service since 2009, based at Komaki Air Base, Nagoya, Japan.

## KC-46 Pegasus

Despite this, the KC-767 found buyers in Italy and Japan. Further political machinations saw the tanker bidding process restarted and this time Boeing won the bid with its KC-46, a similar but improved 767 tanker derivative. The aircraft entered US service in 2019 and examples have been procured by Israel and Italy. Compared with the KC-135 it is intended to supplement and replace, the KC-46 can carry 10 percent more fuel and up to 29.5 tonnes (65,000lb) of cargo. Survivability is improved over the earlier aircraft with the Pegasus featuring infrared countermeasures and limited electronic warfare capabilities.

TRANSPORT AND RECONNAISSANCE

# Embraer C-390 Millennium

Schemed as a jet-powered Hercules replacement, the C-390 flew for the first time in February 2015 and entered service with the Brazilian Air Force in 2019.

Having established an enviable reputation as a manufacturer of light transport and regional airliners, the Brazilian Embraer company sought to develop a medium-sized military transport in the same class as the C-130 Hercules, large numbers of which would be coming to the end of their working lives over the next two decades or so. Support from the Brazilian government was

A Brazilian air force Embraer KC-390 takes part in a demonstration, 2019.

### Embraer C-390

**Weight (maximum take-off):** 86,999kg (191,800lb)
**Dimensions:** Length 35.2m (115ft 6in), Wingspan 35.05m (115ft), Height 11.84m (38ft 10in)
**Powerplant:** Two IAE V2500-E5 turbofans, each rated at 139.4kN (31,330lbf) thrust

**Maximum speed:** 988km/h (614mph)
**Range:** 5020km (3120miles) with 14 tonne payload
**Ceiling:** 11,000m (36,000ft)
**Crew:** 3
**Maximum payload:** 26,000kg (57,000lb)

# TRANSPORT AND RECONNAISSANCE

**Opposite:**
In service with the Brazilian Air Force from 2019, the KC-390 saw much use during the Covid pandemic, flying vaccines and medical supplies to isolated areas.

**Above:**
**Embraer KC-390 Millennium**
This aircraft, serial 26902, from the Portuguese Air Force (FAP), is based at Beja Air Base, July 2024. This is the second of five KC-390 aircraft ordered by FAP in 2019, the first of which was delivered in October 2023.

**Portuguese Air Force Embraer KC-390 transport aircraft during an air display at Beja Air Base.**

enthusiastic and a contract for two prototypes was placed in 2009. Embraer's confidence in the market for its new aircraft appears to have been justified as within five years of the C-390 entering service in Brazil, firm orders had been placed by Austria, the Czech Republic, Hungary, the Netherlands, Portugal and South Korea.

## Export success

From the start, the aircraft was designed with versatility in mind and as well as operating as a straightforward transport, it can be configured as a firefighting aircraft. An airborne tanker variant, designated the KC-390, has also been developed for the Brazilian Air Force.

197

TRANSPORT AND RECONNAISSANCE

# Grumman E-2 Hawkeye

> The first aircraft specifically designed for the AEW role, the E-2 remains the US Navy's standard carrier-based airborne early warning and control platform.

The turboprop-powered E-2 made its first flight in October 1960, intended as a replacement for Grumman's own piston-engined E-1 Tracer. Initial service use with the E-2A from 1964 onwards proved problematic as contemporary electronics were unreliable and consistently overheated, leading to the much-improved E-2B with a different central computer and other changes. There

Photographed on patrol above the Arabian Sea, this E-2C is on the strength of Carrier Airborne Early Warning Squadron (VAW) 116, aboard USS *Nimitz*.

### Grumman E-2C

**Weight (maximum take-off):** 26,082kg (57,500lb)
**Dimensions:** Length 17.60m (57ft 9in), Wingspan 24.56m (80ft 7in), Height 5.58m (18ft 4in)
**Powerplant:** Two 3800kW (5100shp) Allison/Rolls-Royce T56-A-427 turboprop engines

**Maximum speed:** 650km/h (400mph)
**Range:** 2708km (1682 miles)
**Ceiling:** 10,500m (34,700ft)
**Crew:** 5
**Avionics:** Maximum radar detection range approximately 644km (400 miles)

# TRANSPORT AND RECONNAISSANCE

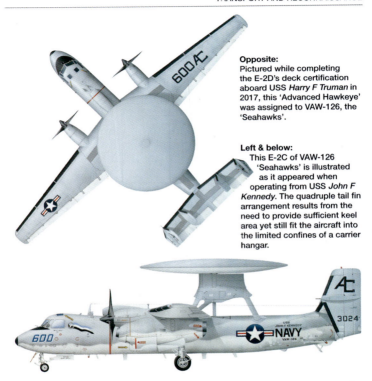

**Opposite:**
Pictured while completing the E-2D's deck certification aboard USS *Harry F Truman* in 2017, this 'Advanced Hawkeye' was assigned to VAW-126, the 'Seahawks'.

**Left & below:**
This E-2C of VAW-126 'Seahawks' is illustrated as it appeared when operating from USS *John F Kennedy*. The quadruple tail fin arrangement results from the need to provide sufficient keel area yet still fit the aircraft into the limited confines of a carrier hangar.

followed decades of upgrades and as of 2025, the aircraft remains in production in E-2D form, the longest production run of any carrier aircraft, serving with five other nations in addition to the USA.

## Operations

Active operational use of the E-2 by the US Navy began during the Vietnam war and it has operated as the 'eyes of the fleet' ever since. The latest E-2D variant is capable of tracking small targets such as portable cruise missiles at up to 550km (340 miles) distance. In addition to its primary role, a carrier-capable transport, the C-2 Greyhound, was developed from the basic E-2 airframe.

TRANSPORT AND RECONNAISSANCE

# Ilyushin Il-76 'Candid'

Developed during the late 1960s, the capable Il-76 has proved highly successful and versatile in both military and civil applications worldwide.

Designed as a strategic assault transport for the Soviet Union, the Il-76 was intended to deliver a 33 tonne payload over a distance of 5000km and to operate from unprepared airstrips. Entering service in June 1974, the aircraft subsequently saw intense use in Afghanistan, delivering nearly three quarters of the total supplies delivered by air and 89% of Soviet troops flown into the country.

The first of the new Il-76MD-90A variant was rolled out in 2012 and is seen appearing at the MAKS air show in July 2013.

## Ilyushin Il-76MD

**Weight (maximum take-off):** 190,000kg (418,878lb)
**Dimensions:** Length 46.59m (152ft 10in), Wingspan 50.5m (165ft 8in), Height 14.76m (48ft 5in)
**Powerplant:** Four Soloviev D-30KP turbofan engines, each rated at 117.7kN (26,500lbf)
**Maximum speed:** 850km/h (528mph)

**Range:** 4200km (2610 miles) with max payload
**Ceiling:** 12,000m (39,370ft)
**Crew:** 6–7
**Armament:** Two 23mm (0.91in) Gryazev-Shipunov GSh-23L cannon flexibly mounted in tail turret
**Maximum payload:** 48,000kg (105,822lb)

TRANSPORT AND RECONNAISSANCE

**Opposite:**
This Il-76M of the Russian Aerospace Forces is shown in the colour scheme typical of the type. The type has formed the backbone of Soviet and Russian airlift capability for the last 50 years.

**Above:**
This Ukrainian Air Force Il-76MD is named Oleksandr Bilyi in honour of the pilot of an Il-76 that was shot down by pro-Russian separatists near Luhansk in 2014.

**Above:**
In July 1993 this Il-78 '34 Blue' arrived at the Royal International Air Tattoo in the UK while simulating refuelling a Tu-95MS 'Bear-S'. The pods containing the refuelling drogues are visible under the wings and on the rear fuselage.

The aircraft remains in service with Russia and 15 other air arms worldwide with the latest variants featuring more efficient, and quieter, Aviadvigatel PS-90 turbofans in place of the original Soloviev D-30s.

## Ilyushin Il-78

As well as serving as a transport, the Il-76 platform has been developed into an airborne tanker, designated the Il-78, as well as the Il-82 radio relay aircraft with a massive 'canoe' fairing above the forward fuselage. In the civil sphere the aircraft has also been developed into an effective firefighting platform capable of carrying up to 49,000 litres of water or retardant.

TRANSPORT AND RECONNAISSANCE

# Kawasaki C-2

A considerably larger development of the C-1 transport, the C-2 can carry four times the payload of the earlier machine up to six times as far.

While looking for a replacement for the C-1, Japan investigated the possibility of acquiring the C-130J Super Hercules, C-17 Globemaster III or Airbus A400M but concluded that no existing design sufficiently fulfilled its requirements, and development of the Kawasaki C-2 (initially known as the C-X) was authorized in 2001. The aircraft's first flight occurred in January 2010 and, despite some delays during

A JASDF C-2 from the 403rd Tactical Airlift Squadron sits on the flightline at Joint Base Elmendorf-Richardson, Alaska, in 2023.

## Kawasaki C-2

**Weight (maximum take-off):** 141,400kg (311,734lb)
**Dimensions:** Length 43.9m (144ft), Wingspan 44.4m (145ft 8in), Height 14.2m (46ft 7in)
**Powerplant:** Two General Electric CF6-80C2K1F turbofan engines, each rated 265.7kN (59,740lbf)

**Maximum speed:** 920km/h (570mph)
**Range:** 7600km (4700 miles) with 20 tonne payload
**Ceiling:** 13,100m (43,000ft)
**Crew:** 3
**Maximum payload:** 37,600kg (82,894lb)

# TRANSPORT AND RECONNAISSANCE

**Opposite top:**
Built at Kawasaki's Gifu factory, this C-2 was delivered to the JASDF in June 2016 and shows the two-tone blue grey camouflage adopted for the type.

**Above:** Roaring into an overcast sky at Naha Air Show in 2018, C-2 '203' shows off the many wheels of the type's rough field undercarriage and its general resemblance to the C-17. The C-2 is smaller than the four-engined C-17 but faster.

development, 22 aircraft were ordered, including the prototype, and production aircraft began to enter service in 2016.

## STOL ability

Although not strictly possessing short take-off and landing (STOL) characteristics, the C-2 was developed with the ability to land and take-off within 500 metres and is able to cruise at Mach 0.8, somewhat faster than the C-17. An electronic intelligence (ELINT) version has also been developed as the RC-2, with a single example entering service in 2022. Kawasaki has actively marketed the aircraft in both military and civil form since 2015, as a competitor to the A400M and Il-76, but by 2025 no export sales had been made.

TRANSPORT AND RECONNAISSANCE

# Leonardo C-27J Spartan

A development of the Fiat G.222, the C-27J was designed to utilize the engines and many of the systems of the C-130J Hercules to maximize commonality between the complementary aircraft.

As a result, the C-27J features Rolls-Royce AE 2100 turboprops and the same 'glass cockpit' as the larger C-130J. Introduced into US service in 2008, only four years later the Spartan fell foul of budget cuts and was retired from US Air Force (USAF) service, despite protests from units operating the C-27J. Some aircraft have enjoyed a second career in the US, however, with 14 Spartans

A Slovak Air Force Leonardo C-27J Spartan takes off at the SIAF Slovak International Air Festival, 2019.

### Leonardo C-27J Spartan

**Weight (maximum take-off):** 32,500kg (71,650lb)
**Dimensions:** Length 22.7m (74ft 6in), Wingspan 28.7m (94ft 2in), Height 9.64m (31ft 8in)
**Powerplant:** Two 3458kW (4637shp) Rolls-Royce AE 2100-D2A turboprops

**Maximum speed:** 602km/h (374mph)
**Range:** 1759km (1093 miles)
**Ceiling:** 9144m (30,000ft)
**Crew:** 2–3
**Maximum payload:** 11,300kg (24,912lb)

# TRANSPORT AND RECONNAISSANCE

**Opposite:**
The Zambian Air Force operates two C-27J Spartans, one of five African nations to fly the type.

**Above:**
The first of the RAAF's fleet of 10 C-27Js was delivered in 2014, the type having been selected to replace the veteran DHC-4 Caribou. Australia's C-27Js are operated by No. 35 Squadron.

**Right:** Slovakia operates two C-27Js allocated to the 46th Wing based at Malacky Air Base.

serving with the US Coast Guard and another seven utilized by United States Army Special Operations Aviation Command.

## Export orders

The C-27J has enjoyed success on the international market and serves with 17 nations. The aircraft remains in production in 2025 and has been developed into variants optimized for the electronic intelligence (ELINT) role as the EC-27 'Jedi' and as the MC-27J gunship equipped with a 30mm (1.18in) weapon firing laterally from the fuselage port side. Both these variants serve with the Italian air force. The aircraft possesses a sprightly performance and exceptional agility for a transport; examples have regularly been looped and rolled during air show demonstrations.

TRANSPORT AND RECONNAISSANCE

# Lockheed C-5 Galaxy

By a considerable margin the largest transport aircraft in the US Air Force (USAF) inventory, the C-5 Galaxy has remained in constant service since 1969.

A hugely expensive project, the Galaxy suffered from costly developmental problems, threatening the future of the whole programme and nearly causing the demise of Lockheed itself, the company only surviving as a result of government loans. Initially, structural issues with the wing restricted payload capability but a new wing design was developed in the late 1970s and the entire fleet retrofitted during the 1980s.

A USAF Lockheed C-5 Galaxy aircraft arrives at the Stuttgart Army Airfield, Germany, on 2 March 2016.

### Lockheed C-5M

**Weight (maximum take-off):** 381,018kg (840,000lb)
**Dimensions:** Length 75.31m (247ft 1in), Wingspan 67.89m (222ft 9in), Height 19.84m (65ft 1in)
**Powerplant:** Four General Electric F138-100 turbofan engines, each rated at 230kN (51,000lbf) thrust

**Maximum speed:** 856km/h (532mph)
**Range:** 8900km (5500 miles) with a 54,431kg (120,000lb) payload
**Ceiling:** 12,500m (41,100ft)
**Crew:** Typically 7
**Maximum payload:** 127,459kg (281,000lb)

## TRANSPORT AND RECONNAISSANCE

**Opposite:**
This C-5A is pictured as it appeared when it entered service in 1972. This Galaxy suffered a mid-air fire in 1988 but was repaired and returned to service until it was finally scrapped in 2013.

**Above:** This C-5B Galaxy of the USAF's 436th Military Airlift Wing wears the European One 'lizard' camouflage scheme of the 1980s.

**Right:** A USAF C-5M Super Galaxy takes off from Travis Air Force Base, California, March 2022.

## Strategic transport

Subsequently, the C-5 has matured into a far more satisfactory strategic transport and in its current form as the C-5M 'Super Galaxy' has received more efficient and powerful engines, allowing for the carriage of a greater payload over longer distances. The C-5M fleet in 2025 comprised 52 aircraft, offering a payload capability unmatched by any other Western military transport, the only comparable aircraft currently flying worldwide being the slightly shorter An-124. In September 2009 a C-5M claimed 41 records set during a single flight, including carrying a payload of more than 80,000kg to an altitude greater than 12,500m (41,100ft).

TRANSPORT AND RECONNAISSANCE

# Lockheed C-130 Hercules

Production of the Hercules, one of the most successful aircraft of all time, began in 1954 and was ongoing in 2025: the longest production run of any military aircraft.

Lockheed took quite a gamble on the success of the Hercules and it is fair to say it paid off: the C-130 has served the US since 1956 and has been operated by the militaries of an astonishing 74 nations, most of which retain the aircraft in their inventory. Over 2500 have been built to date. Current production aircraft are built to C-130J Super Hercules standard featuring Rolls-Royce AE

A C-130J Super Hercules takes off from the Farnborough Aerodrome runway in July 2010.

## Lockheed C-130J Hercules

**Weight (maximum take-off):** 70,300kg (155,000lb)
**Dimensions:** Length 29.79m (97ft 9in), Wingspan 40.41m (132ft 7in), Height 11.84m (38ft 10in)
**Powerplant:** Four 3458kW (4637shp) Rolls-Royce AE 2100D3 turboprop engines

**Maximum speed:** 670kmh (417mph)
**Range:** 2070km (1290 miles) with 15 tonne (16.5 ton) payload
**Ceiling:** 8600m (28,000ft) with 19 tonne (21 ton) payload
**Crew:** 3
**Maximum payload:** 19,051kg (42,000lb)

## TRANSPORT AND RECONNAISSANCE

**Opposite:**
The large antennae on the sides of the tailfin identify this aircraft as an EC-130J Commando Solo psychological operations platform. Commando Solo aircraft were used operationally during the Libyan civil war (2015).

**Above & below:**
The Hercules transport has been used for many purposes, but the most dramatic is likely its transformation into the astonishingly heavily armed AC-130 gunship, as demonstrated by this AC-130H Spectre, which carries a 105mm (4.13in) cannon and 40mm (1.57in) Gatling guns.

2100 turboprops equipped with six-bladed propellers in place of the Allison T56 units previously fitted.

As well as its service as a conventional military transport, the Hercules has been adapted for a number of other roles including the MC-130 for Special Operations, the EC-130 for electronic warfare and electronic intelligence (ELINT), the KC-130 tanker and the fearsomely armed AC-130 gunship variants. The Hercules has also seen considerable civil use, large numbers serving with the US Coast Guard as well as several fitted out as firefighting aircraft.

TRANSPORT AND RECONNAISSANCE

# Lockheed U-2

> The high-altitude U-2, which became world famous during the Cold War after an example was shot down over the Soviet Union in 1960, remains in US Air Force (USAF) service today.

Initially a CIA programme, the U-2 was derived from the high-speed F-104 Starfighter and developed in great secrecy. Intended to operate at 21,000m (70,000ft), which was believed to render it immune to Soviet defence systems and beyond the range of Soviet radar, many overflights of Soviet territory were made before a U-2 flown by Francis Gary Powers was shot down and Powers interned.

A U-2 takes-off for a Weapons School Integration mission at Nellis Air Force Base, Nevada, in 2021.

## Lockheed U-2S

**Weight (maximum take-off):** 18,144kg (40,000lb)
**Dimensions:** Length 19.2m (63ft), Wingspan 31m (103ft), Height 4.88m (16ft)
**Powerplant:** One General Electric F118-101 turbofan engine, rated at 76kN (17,000lbf) thrust

**Maximum speed:** 805km/h (500mph)
**Range:** 11,280km (7010 miles)
**Ceiling:** 24,000m (80,000ft)
**Crew:** 1
**Payload:** Up to 2300kg (5000lb) of cameras or sensors

## TRANSPORT AND RECONNAISSANCE

**Opposite:**
The U-2A was the initial production type, powered by a Pratt & Whitney J57-P-37A engine; 48 were built.

**Above:**
The CIA's Project Aquatone saw civil-registered U-2s conduct reconnaissance overflights of the Soviet Union as well as flying sorties over Cuba during the 1962 Missile Crisis.

**Above:**
Designed for standoff tactical reconnaissance in Europe, the U-2R is a larger and more capable aircraft. A distinguishing feature of these aircraft is the large instrumentation 'superpod' under each wing.

## High-altitude ability

Despite this convincing display of its vulnerability, the aircraft's high altitude performance remains unique and the ability of a U-2 to reconnoitre a site at much shorter notice than is required for a satellite has resulted in the retention of the U-2 within the US inventory. U-2s have operated over Cuba, Vietnam, Iraq and other locations of interest and remain active today with several USAF reconnaissance wings. A handful of U-2s are also operated as civil high-altitude research aircraft by NASA. Total U-2 production amounted to 104 aircraft, of which 27 U-2s remain active with the USAF in 2025.

TRANSPORT AND RECONNAISSANCE

# Shaanxi Y-8 and KJ-200

The Y-8 started life as a reverse-engineered Chinese-built Antonov An-12, but subsequent development resulted in an aircraft quite distinct from its Soviet progenitor.

China imported a few An-12s and a manufacturing licence during the 1960s but the Sino-Soviet split resulted in the withdrawal of technical assistance from the USSR and the aircraft was prepared for production through a process of reverse engineering. The first Chinese-built aircraft flew in 1972 and Y-8s began to be serial manufactured in 1981, immediately

Chinese paratroopers jump from a Y-8 aircraft during a Pakistan–China military exercise in Jhelum in November 2011.

### Shaanxi KJ-200H

**Weight (maximum take-off):** 61,000kg (134,100lb)
**Dimensions:** Length 34m (111ft 6in), Wingspan 38m (124ft 7in), Height 11.16m (36ft 7in)
**Powerplant:** Four Zhuzhou WoJiang WJ-6 turboprops, each developing 3126kW (4192hp)
**Maximum speed:** 660km/h (410mph)

**Range:** 5615km (3489 miles)
**Ceiling:** 10,400m (34,120ft)
**Crew:** 5
**Capacity:** 96 troops or 82 paratroops, or up to 60 medevac patients
**Armament:** Two 23mm (0.91in) cannon

# TRANSPORT AND RECONNAISSANCE

**Opposite:**
This typically filthy Y-8C was observed at Zhengzhou International Airport in April 2023.

**Above:**
Flying with CAAC Airlines, this civil Y-8F-100 was spotted at Hanzhong, China, in June 2023.

**Above:**
The KJ-200B features a SATCOM antenna on top of its forward fuselage, a new AEW&C antenna in the nose, side-looking ESM antennas on its rear fuselage and ESM antenna on top of its tail fin.

identifiable by its more pointed nose glazing, derived from that fitted to the H-6 bomber.

## Multirole aircraft

The basic aircraft has been modified to fulfil a wide variety of roles as well as tactical transport. Y-8 variants serve as electronic intelligence (ELINT) platforms, in the ASW role with prominent tail mounted MAD boom and as airborne tankers, among other roles. In the AEW role, the aircraft carries a large AESA radar in a prominent fairing above the fuselage and is designated the KJ-200. An export AEW variant with a rotodome resembling a scaled-down version of that on the E-3 Sentry has been delivered to Pakistan.

TRANSPORT AND RECONNAISSANCE

# Shaanxi Y-9 and KJ-500

A modernized, stretched and upgraded development of the Y-8, the Y-9 is intended to compete with the C-130J Super Hercules but has so far attracted few customers.

Produced in collaboration with Antonov, designers of the An-12 which the Y-9 circuitously derives from, the Y-9 was originally known as the Y-8X but differed sufficiently from previous iterations of the Y-8 that the aircraft received a totally new designation. The first flight was made in November 2010 and the Y-9 achieved full operating capability with the People's Liberation Army Air Force (PLAAF) at

A Y-9 makes a practice flight before Airshow China 2021 in Zhuhai, Guangdong, China.

### Shaanxi Y-9

**Weight (maximum take-off):** 265,352kg (585,000lb)
**Dimensions:** Length 36.07m (118ft 4in), Wingspan 38m (124ft 8in), Height 11.3m (37ft 1in)
**Powerplant:** Four WoJiang WJ-6C turboprop engines each rated at 3805kW (5103hp)

**Maximum speed:** 650km/h (400mph)
**Range:** 2200km (1400 miles) with 15,000kg (33,069lb) payload
**Ceiling:** 10,400m (34,100ft)
**Crew:** 4
**Capacity:** 98 paratroopers, 72 medevac patients or 20,000kg (44,092lb) of cargo

TRANSPORT AND RECONNAISSANCE

**Opposite:**
Seen at Zhuhai Airshow in 2021, this Y-9L is adapted for the medical evacuation role and is operated by the 4th Transport Division.

**Above:**
The regular Y-9 is a transport aircraft much better suited to the needs of the PLAAF in the 21st century than the Y-8. It can carry almost twice as much fuel as the earlier aircraft and is easily identified by the auxiliary fins on the horizontal tailplane.

**Above:**
The KJ-500A is an improved variant easily identified by its aerial refuelling probe. This aircraft was seen at Zhuhai Jinwan Airport, China, in November 2022.

the end of 2017. The aircraft features the cockpit design of later Y-8 variants, dispenses with the rear turret, and is equipped with a full 'glass cockpit' enabling it to be operated by a crew of two.

## Adaptable type

Despite its relatively recent appearance, the Y-9, like the Y-8 before it, has already been adapted to a number of roles with the Y-9JZ electronic intelligence (ELINT) platform, KQ-200 maritime patrol aircraft and KJ-500 AEW&C variant all in service in China. The latter carries a non-rotating pylon-mounted circular radome containing three AESA radar arrays giving full 360° coverage.

TRANSPORT AND RECONNAISSANCE

# ShinMaywa US-1 and US-2

> One of very few flying boats still in regular service, the 21st-century US-2 ultimately derives from the PS-1, developed in the 1960s for the anti-submarine warfare (ASW) role.

The Shin Meiwa PS-1 was withdrawn in 1989 but its air-sea rescue variant the US-1A remained in service with the Japan Maritime Self-Defence Force (JMSDF) until 2017 and is credited with rescuing 827 people. Due to its success an improved and updated model was developed, culminating in the first flight of the new US-2 in 2003, by which time the manufacturer had been renamed ShinMaywa.

Caught 'on the step' during its take-off run, this is one of the JMSDF's new US-2 amphibians. Note the six-bladed propellers.

### ShinMaywa US-2

**Weight (maximum take-off):** 47,700kg (105,160lb)
**Dimensions:** Length 33.46m (109ft 9in), Wingspan 33.15m (108ft 9in), Height 9.8m (32ft 2in)
**Powerplant:** Four 3424kW (4592hp) Rolls-Royce AE 2100J turboprops

**Maximum speed:** 560km/h (350mph)
**Range:** 4700km (2900 miles)
**Ceiling:** 7195m (23,606ft)
**Crew:** 11 (2 pilots, 1 search-and-rescue coordinator, 2 on-board maintenance personnel, 3 divers, 2 paramedics and 1 sensor operator)
**Armament:** None

TRANSPORT AND RECONNAISSANCE

**All images:**
One of 14 Shin Meiwa US-1A amphibians built for the air-sea rescue role, this example was operated by the 71st Hikotai at Iwakuni in Yamaguchi Prefecture, Japan. The 71st Hikotai also flies the later US-2.

## US-2

The US-2, which entered service in 2009, differs from the earlier model primarily in its powerplant, with four Rolls-Royce AE 2100J fitted with six-bladed propellers replacing the General Electric T64s of the earlier aircraft. The only variant so far to enter service is the basic ASR version but ShinMaywa has been actively marketing the aircraft for other roles. A firefighting variant has been proposed and this is under consideration by Greece to replace its current firefighting fleet. In addition, a maritime patrol variant has been marketed to India, Thailand and Indonesia.

TRANSPORT AND RECONNAISSANCE

# Xi'an Y-20 'Kunpeng'

China's newest strategic transport, the highly capable Y-20 design was launched in the early 2000s and the aircraft has been in production since 2013.

Following difficulties in obtaining sufficient numbers of Il-76 transport aircraft from Russia, development of an indigenous Chinese transport of similar size was given high priority. The Y-20 benefitted from consultation with the Ukrainian Antonov company during the design phase and the aircraft flew in January 2013. Compared to the Il-76, the Y-20 features a more aerodynamically

An early Y-20 is demonstrated during Airshow China 2018 at Zuihai.

### Xi'an Y-20A

**Weight (maximum take-off):** 180,000kg (396,832lb)
**Dimensions:** Length 47m (154ft 2in), Wingspan 50m (164ft 1in), Height 15m (49ft 3in)
**Powerplant:** Four Soloviev D-30KP-2 turbofan engines, each rated at 117.68kN (26,460lb)
**Maximum speed:** Mach 0.75

**Range:** 7800km (4800 miles) with payload of two main battle tanks
**Ceiling:** 13,000m (43,000ft)
**Crew:** 3
**Capacity:** 300 troops, 110 paratroopers, 200 medevac patients or equivalent cargo load

# TRANSPORT AND RECONNAISSANCE

**Opposite:**
Y-20s remain a comparatively rare sight in the West but this example flew into Innsbruck Airport, Austria, in early 2023.

**Above:**
An early-production Y-20, on the strength of the 12th Air Regiment. The aircraft is based at Chengdu-Qionglai in southwest China.

A Y-20 taxies at Halim Perdana Kusuma Airport, Jakarta, Indonesia. By 2025, around 80 examples of the Y-20 had been built, all for use by the PLAAF, but the aircraft is being actively marketed for export.

advanced wing design conferring greater range than the Russian aircraft and features extensive use of composite materials to reduce weight.

## Cargo compartment

The cargo compartment is both wider and taller than the Il-76, allowing bulkier loads to be carried, including main battle tanks. The initial Y-20A was officially introduced into Chinese service in 2016, followed by an inflight refuelling tanker variant, the YY-20A. The Y-20B, featuring more powerful Shenyang WS-20 turbofans, appeared during 2020 along with a similarly powered tanker derivative, the YY-20B. Sixty-seven Y-20 aircraft were known to have been delivered by the end of 2023 and production of the Y-20 is ongoing.

# INDEX

Note: page numbers in **bold** refer to information contained in captions.

*Admiral Kuznetsov* (aircraft carrier) 78–9, **102–3**
Aermacchi M-346 Master/Yakovlev Yak-130 'Mitten' 110–11, **110–11**, 128–9, **129**
Aero L-39 Albatros 112–13, **112–13**, 114
Aero L-39 Skyfox 113
Aero L-159 ALCA 114–15, **114–15**
Afghan Air Force **123**
Afghanistan **28**, 31, 65, 125, 135, 139, 141, 154–5, 161, 300
AIDC F-CK-1 Ching Kuo 12–13, **12–13**
Air National Guard **51**, **125**, **193**
Airbus A310 airliner 176
Airbus A330 MRTT 176, 177, **177**
Airbus A400M Atlas 172–3, **172–3**, 202, 203
Airbus C-295 174–5, **174–5**
Airbus MRTT 176–7, **176–7**, 194
Angola **25**, 73, 75, 123
Antonov 214, 218
Antonov An-8 'Camp' 178
Antonov An-12 'Cub' 178–9, **178–9**, 212, 214
Antonov An-24 180–1
Antonov An-26 'Curl' 180–1, **180–1**
Antonov An-124 Ruslan 'Condor' 182–3, **182–3**
Australia 24, 53, 59, 61, 63, 117, 177, 190, 191

BAE Systems Hawk 14–15, **15**
Bangladesh **147**
Belarus **77**
Belgian Air Force **173**
Belgium 25, **115**, **121**, 140
Beriev A-50 'Mainstay' 184–5, **184–5**
Beriev KJ-2000 'Mainring' 184–5, **185**
Boeing 707 176, 188, 192
Boeing 737 116, 190–1
Boeing 767 194, **195**
Boeing B-52 Stratofortress 118–19, **118–19**, 158
Boeing C-17 Globemaster III 172, 186–7, **186–7**, 202, **203**
Boeing C-135 Stratolifter 192
Boeing C-141 Starlifter 186, 192
Boeing E-3 Sentry 184, 188–9, **188–9**, 190, 213

Boeing E-7 Wedgetail **189**, 190–1, **190–1**
Boeing KC-45 177
Boeing KC-46 Pegasus 194–5, **194–5**
Boeing KC-135 Stratotanker 176, 177, **191**, 192–3, **192–3**, 194, 195
Boeing KC-767 194–5, **195**
Boeing P-8 Poseidon 93, 116–17, **116–17**, 133, 137, **137**, 163
Boeing RC-135 Rivet Joint 192–3
Brazil 86, **87**, 89, 122, **122**, 196–7
Brazilian Air Force 123, **123**, 196–7
Breguet 144

CAC/PAC JF-17 Thunder 16–17, **16–17**
Canada 41, 53, **58–9**, 59, 86, 117, 121, **121**, 137, 140, 176–7, **187**
CASA C-212 174
CASA/IPTN CN-235 174–5
Changchun Air Show **126**
Chechnya 157, 161
Chengdu J-7/F-7 'Fishbed'/'Fishcan' 16, 18–19, **18–19**, 21, 43
Chengdu J-10 'Firebird' 20–1, **20–1**, 23
Chengdu J-20 'Fagin' 22–3, **22**, **23**, 51, 94, 97
Chengdu JJ-5 126
China 12, 16–23, 42, 51, 91–4, **93**, 97, 99, 101–5, 126–7, **127**, **129**, 146–7, **147**, 166, 168, **169**, 179, 181, **181**, 184–5, **185**, 212, **213**, 218
China Aviation Industry Conference and Nanchang Air Show **128**
Chinese Navy 93, 103, 128, **129**, 167, 168–9
Cold War 7, 24, 51, 118, 136, 143, **155**, 158, 161, 210
Colombia 47, **195**
Croatia 149
Cuba 73, **75**, 211, **211**
Cuban Missile Crisis **211**
Czech Republic 112, 114–15, **115**, **155**, 197
Czechoslovak Air Force **113**, 114

Dassault Mirage 5 24–5, **25**
Dassault Mirage 2000 13, 28–9, **28–9**
Dassault Mirage II 24
Dassault Mirage III 24–5, **24**, 28
Dassault Mirage F1 26–7
Dassault Mirage F2 26
Dassault Rafaele 30–1, **30–1**
Dassault/Dornier Alpha Jet 120–1, **120–1**

# INDEX

DHC-4 Caribou **205**
Douglas TA-4J Skyhawk 15
drones 8, 29, 63

East Germany 77
Ecuador 145
Ecuadorian Air Force (FAE) **47**
Egypt 25, 29, 81, 97, 123
Electra airliners 136
Embraer A-29 Super Tucano 123
Embraer AT-27 123
Embraer C-390 Millennium 196–7, **196–7**
Embraer EMB 312 Tucano 122–3, **123**
Embraer EMB 314 Super Tucano 122–3, **122–2**
Embraer KC-390 197
Embraer T-27 trainer 123
Eritrea 99
Ethiopia 75, 99
Eurofighter Typhoon 30, 32–3, **32–3**, **35**, 89
Europrop 173

Fairchild A-10 Thunderbolt II 124–5, **124–5**
Fairchild OA-10 **125**
Fiat G.222 204
France 25, 29, 30, 120, 121, 123, 144, 145, **173**, 177, 189
French Air Force 28–31, **29**, **120**, **144**

General Dynamics F-16 Fighting Falcon 12, 16–17, 48, 49, 52, 58, 59, 76, 84–5, **85**
  enlarged (Agile Falcon) 85
  General Dynamics F-16 Fighting Falcon F-16C Block 50 89
  General Dynamics F-16A/B Fighting Falcon 34–5, **34–5**, 36
  General Dynamics F-16C/D Fighting Falcon 36–7, **36–7**
General Dynamics F-16XL 69
General Dynamics F-111 Aardvark **61**, 68–9, 142
General Dynamics X-62A VISTA 37
General Dynamics/Lockheed Martin F-16E/F Desert Falcon 37–8, **38–9**
General Dynamics/Lockheed Martin F-16V Viper 37–8
General Electric 46, 217
*George Washington* (aircraft carrier) **62**
Georgia 157, 161
Germany 32–3, 41, 117, 120–1, 140–1, 176–7, 189
Greece 29, 57, 217
Grenada 125

Grumman C-2 Greyhound 199
Grumman E-1 Tracer 198
Grumman E-2 Hawkeye 198–9, **198–9**
Grumman EA-6B Prowler 62
Grumman F-14 Tomcat 27, 40–1, **40–1**, 58, **61**
Guizhou FTC-2000 42–3, **42**
Guizhou JL-9 42–3, **42–3**
Gulf War
  first 29, 37, 65, **65**, 69, 125, 135, **141**, 145, **145**, 151, 153
  second 125, 139, 141

Hal Tejas 44–5, **44–5**, **73**
Hal Tejas Mk II 45
Hongdu JL-8/Karakorum K-8 126–7, **126–7**
Hongdu JL-9 128
Hongdu JL-10 and L-15 128–9, **128–9**
Hungarian Air Force **89**

IAI F-21 47
IAI Kfir 46–7, **46–7**
Ilyushin Il-18 130
Ilyushin Il-38 'May' 130–1, **130–1**, 163
Ilyushin Il-76 'Candid' 200–1, **200–1**, 203, 218
Ilyushin Il-76MD 184–5
Ilyushin Il-78 201
India 14, 29, 31, 73, **73**, **75**, 77, 101, 106, 117, 131, **131**, 145, **145**, 185, 217
Indian Air Force (IAF) 29, 44–5, **44–5**, **73**, **100**, **145**
Indonesia 15, **15**, 99, 105, 174, 217, **219**
Iran 21, 26–7, 40, 41, **41**, 57, 86, 87, 105, 151, 153
Iran-Iraq war 26–7, 41, **41**, 155
Iraq 17, 31, 41, **63**, 65, **68**, 153, 187, 211
Iraqi Air Force 115, **115**
Islamic State of Iraq and the Levant (ISIL) 51, 115, **115**, **191**
Israel 25, 35, 38, **44**, 46–7, **46**, 49, 69, **73**, 75, 195
Israel Aircraft Industries **195**
Italian Air Force **35**, 111
Italian Navy 55, 64–5
Italy 32, 53, 140, 141, 195

Japan 41, **57**, 65, 67, 84–5, 137, 195, **195**, 202, **217**
Japan Air Self-Defense Force (JASDF) **84**, 85, **195**, 202, **202–3**, **216**
Japanese Maritime Self Defence Force (JMSDF) 132, 216

# INDEX

Kai EA-50 48–9
Kai F-50 49
Kai FA-50 Fighting Eagle 49
Kai RA-50 48–9
Kai T-50 Golden Eagle 48–9, **48–9**
Kawasaki C-1 202
Kawasaki C-2 132–3, 202–3, **202–3**
Kawasaki P-1 132–3, **132–3**
Kubinka airshow **79, 111**
Kuwait 33, 59, 61, 135

Leonardo C-27J Spartan 204–5, **204–5**
Libya 25, **25**, 31, 33, **74**, 153
Libyan civil war **209**
Lockheed C-5 Galaxy 182, 186, 206–7, **206–7**
Lockheed C-130 Hercules 172, 178, 179, 186, 196, 202, 204, 208–9, **208–9**, 214
Lockheed EC-121 Warning Star 188
Lockheed F-104 Starfighter 12, 140, 210
Lockheed F-117 Night Hawk 134–5, **134–5**
Lockheed Martin 84–5
Lockheed Martin F-22 Raptor 7, **8**, 50–1, **50–1**, 67, 70, 71, 106
Lockheed Martin F-35 Lightning II 7, 70, 71, 96, 124, 125
    Lockheed Martin F-35A Lightning II **7**, 52–3, **52–3**, 54, 55
    Lockheed Martin F-35B/C Lightning II 54–5, **54–5**, 65
Lockheed Martin X-35 52
Lockheed Martin YF-22 **51**
Lockheed Martin YF-23 50
Lockheed P-3 Orion 116, 132, **133**, 136–7, **136–7**
Lockheed Super Constellation 188
Lockheed U-2 210–11, **210–11**
'Loyal Wingman' drones 8
Luftwaffe **32**, 33, 120–1, 141
    see also German Air Force

MAKS airshow **80**, **105**, **106**, **200**
Malaysia 15, **15**, 59
McDonnell Douglas AV-8B Harrier II 52, 54, 64–5, **64–5**
McDonnell Douglas F-4 Phantom II 34, 40, 56–7, **56–7**, 68
McDonnell Douglas F-4E Terminator 2020 57
McDonnell Douglas F-15A-C Eagle 48, 66–7, **66–7**, 76, 98, **192**
McDonnell Douglas F-15E 'Strike Eagle' 68–9, **68–9**, 70, **71**, 99

McDonnell Douglas F/A-18 Hornet 12, **26**, 52, 58–9, **58–9**
McDonnell Douglas T-45 Goshawk 15
McDonnell Douglas/Boeing EA-18 Growler 62–3, **62–3**
McDonnell Douglas/Boeing F-15EX Eagle II 70–1, **70–1**
McDonnell Douglas/Boeing F/A-18 Super Hornet 59, 60–1, **60–1**, 62, 63
Mexican Navy **175**
Mikoyan Gurevich MiG-15 148
Mikoyan Gurevich MiG-17 34, 126, 148
Mikoyan Gurevich MiG-19 146
Mikoyan Gurevich MiG-21 'Fishbed' 18, 42–3, 44, 72–3, **72–3**, 74, 90
Mikoyan Gurevich MiG-23 'Flogger' 74–5, **74–5**
Mikoyan Gurevich MiG-25 'Foxbat' 82, **82**
Mikoyan Gurevich MiG-29 'Fulcrum' **17**, 49, 76–7, **76–7**, 78, 99
Mikoyan Gurevich MiG-29K 78–9, **78–9**, 80–1
Mikoyan Gurevich MiG-29M 80–1, **81**
Mikoyan Gurevich MiG-31 'Foxhound' 82–3, **82–3**
Mikoyan Gurevich MiG-35 Fulcrum 80–1, **80–1**
Mikoyan MiG-27 **75**
Mil Mi-25 41
Mirage F1AZ **27**
Mirage F1CZ **27**
Mirage III 16, 46
Mirage V 16
Mitsubishi F-1 84
Mitsubishi F-2 84–5, **84–5**
Multi Role Combat Aircraft (MRCA) 140–1
Myanmar 17, **17**, 19, 43, 126, 127, 147, **147**

Nanchang A-5 'Fantan' (Nanchang Q-5) 146–7, **147**
Netherlands 53, 86, 140, 197
New Zealand 117
Nigeria 17, 121, 145
*Nimitz* (aircraft carrier) **198**
North American A-5 Vigilante 16
North American T-2 Buckeye 15
North Korea 19, 73, 75, 147
Northrop, Jack 138
Northrop B-2 Spirit 138–9, **138–9**, 142
Northrop B-35 138
Northrop B-49 138
Northrop F-5 12, 86–7, **86–7**
Northrop F/A-18 35

## INDEX

Northrop YF-17 35, 58
Northrop YF-23 50

Pakistan 16–17, **16–17**, 19, 20–1, 25, **25**, 97, 126–7, **147**, 213
Pakistan Air Force 126
Panavia Tornado 140–1, **140–1**
People's Liberation Army Air Force (PLAAF) 19–20, **21**, 22, **23**, 42, **43**, 91–2, **92–3**, 94–6, **97**, **105**, 126, **127**, 129, **129**, 147, **147**, **167**, 168–9, **169**, 181, **185**, 214, **215**, **219**
Peruvian Air Force **29**
Polish Air Force **76**, 150, **175**

Republic of China Air Force (ROCAF) 12
Republic F-84 Thunderjet 148
Republic of Singapore Air Force (RSAF) **141**
Rockwell B-1 Lancer 142–3, **142–3**
Rolls-Royce **55**, 119, 149, 169, 204, 208–9, 217
Romania 148–9
Royal Air Force (RAF) 33, 55, **69**, 115, **125**, 141, **141**, **145**, **173**, **176**, 189, **189**, **191**
'Red Arrows' **15**
Royal Australian Air Force (RAAF) **14**, **24**, **61**, 63, **177**, 190, **190–1**, **205**
Royal Bahraini Air Force **39**
Royal Canadian Air Force (RCAF) **187**
Royal Jordanian Air Force **39**
Royal Malaysian Air Force **15**
Royal New Zealand Air Force (RNZAF) 137
Royal Thai Air Force **49**
Russia 8, 23, 33, **79**, 81, 94, 98, 99, 101, 104, 106–7, 131, 153–4, **155**, **156**, 157, 159, 161, 163, 166, **166**, **168**, 178–9, 181, 183, **183**, 184, **185**, 201, **201**, 218, 219
*see also* Soviet Union
Russian Aerospace Forces **81**, 83, 107, 153, 155, 158, 178, 182, **184**, 185, **201**
Russian Air Force **77**, 105, **152**, **178–9**
Russian Naval Aviation 178
Russian Navy 79, **79**, 83, **101**, **102**, 103, **130–1**, 163, **181**

Saab JAS 39 Gripen 86, 88–9, **88–9**
Saab Viggen **45**, 88
Saudi Arabia 33, 67, 69, 71, **71**, 141, **141**, 189
SEPECAT Jaguar 144–5, **144–5**
Serbia **77**, 149, **149**
Serbian Air Force **148**, 149
Shaanxi KJ-200 **97**, 212–13, **213**
Shaanxi KJ-500 214–15, **215**

Shaanxi KJ-2000 **97**
Shaanxi Y-8 212–13, **212–13**, 214–15, **215**
Shaanxi Y-9 214–15, **214–15**
Shenyang F-6 147
Shenyang FC-31 Gyrfalcon 97
Shenyang J-6 'Farmer' 146–7
Shenyang J-8 'Finback' 90–1, **90–1**
Shenyang J-11 'Flanker-B+' 92–3, **92–3**, 103
Shenyang J-11BS trainer 93, 94
Shenyang J-15 102–3
Shenyang J-16 94–5, **94–5**
Shenyang J-31/J-35 51, 96–7, **96–7**
Shin Meiwa PS-1 216
ShinMaywa US-1 216–17, **217**
ShinMaywa US-2 216–17, **216**
Soko IAR-93 Vultur 149
Soko J-22 Orao 148–9, **148–9**
South African Air Force (SAAF) **27**
South Korea 48, 49, 69, 86, 87, 117, 191
Soviet Union (USSR) 7, 18, 76, **77**, 79–81, **81**, **83**, 98–9, 102–4, 110, 112, 114, 131, **131**, 136–7, 139, 146, 148, 150, **151**, 152, **153**, 155, 158, **161**, 163–5, **165**, 178, **179**, 181–2, **183**, 184, 200, **201**, 210, **211**, 212, 300
Spain **26**, 27, 32, 59
STOL (Short Take Off and Landing) 174, 203
STOVL (Short Take Off and Vertical Landing) 54
Sukhoi Su-17 150–1, **151**
Sukhoi Su-22 'Fitter' 49, 150–1, **150–1**
Sukhoi Su-24 'Fencer' 152–3, **152–3**
Sukhoi Su-25 'Frogfoot' **17**, 154–5, **154–5**
Sukhoi Su-27 'Flanker' 76, 92, 98–9, **98–9**, 100, 104, 107, 156, **157**
Sukhoi Su-30 'Flanker' 100–1, **100–1**
Sukhoi Su-30MK 101
Sukhoi Su-30MKK 95, 101
Sukhoi Su-33 'Flanker-D' 102–3, **102–3**
Sukhoi Su-34 'Fullback' 156–7, **156–7**
Sukhoi Su-35 'Flanker-E/M' 104–5, **104–5**
Sukhoi Su-57 'Felon' 23, 51, 104, 106–7, **106–7**
Sukhoi T8-1D 154
Sukhoi T8-3 154
Sukhoi T-10-1 98–9

Taiwan 12–13, 29, 39
Tupolev Tu-16 166
Tupolev Tu-22 'Blinder' 160
Tupolev Tu-22M3 'Backfire' 160–1, **160–1**
Tupolev Tu-95 'Bear' 33, 158–9, **158–9**, 162, **162**

INDEX

Tupolev Tu-142 'Bear' 162–3, **162–3**
Tupolev Tu-160 'Blackjack' 164–5, **164–5**

Ukraine War 8, 81, 83, 99, **99**, 105, 107, 153, 154, 155, **155**, 157, 159, 161, 165, **181, 185**
United Kingdom (UK) 32–3, 89, 117, **125**, 144, 177, 191
United States 12, 16, 27, **31, 41**, 76, 86, **86**, 123, 125, **127**, 158, 184, 186, 187, 191, 199, 204
United States Air Force (USAF) **7, 37**, 47, 50, **50, 52–3**, 53, 56–7, **56**, 67–71, **67, 69–70**, 115, 118, **119**, 135, **139**, 143, 177, 186, **186**, 188–90, **188**, 192–4, **192–3, 195**, 204, 206, **206–7**, 210–11
    Lightweight Fighter Program 34–5, 58
United States Marine Corps 54–7, **55**, 59, **59, 61**, 64, **64**

United States Navy 15, 31, 40, 55–61, **61**, 63–5, **63, 86**, 93, **116**, 117, 136–7, **136, 137**, 161, 198–9

Vietnam 99, 107, 113, 211

Xi'an H-6 'Badger' **105**, 166–7, 213
Xi'an JH-7 'Flounder' 168–9, **168–9**
Xi'an KJ-3000 185
Xi'an Y-7 181, **181**
    Xi'an Y-7H 181, **181**
Xi'an Y-20 'Kunpeng' **97**, 185, 218–19, **218–19**

Yakovlev Yak-130 'Mitten' 110–11, **110–11**, 128–9, **129**

# Picture Credits

Alamy: 12 (Associated Press), 42 (ZUMA Press), 91 (Imaginechina), 94 (James Hancock), 148 (VDWI Aviation), 149 (Dean West), 176 (Stocktrek Images)

Creative Commons Attribution-Share Alike 2.0 Generic Licence: 111 (Mashley Morgan), 132 (Ken H), 146 (Faisal Akram)

Creative Commons Attribution-Share Alike 4.0 International Licence: 133 (JMSDF), 195, 216 (JMSDF)

Dreamstime: 10 (Upadek), 14 (Ryan Fletcher), 16 (Umair Sharif), 26 (David Acosta Alleky), 30 (Ryan Fletcher), 44 (Ninlawan Donlakkham), 45 (Vishwa Kiran), 46 (VanderWolfImages), 48 (Gilang Putraditya Purba), 49 (Poonsak Pornnatwuttiku), 78 & 80 (Artyomanikeev), 82 (Viewside), 86 (Amichaelbrown), 98 (Fotogenix), 104 & 110 (Artyomanikeev), 112 (Bdingman), 113 & 120 (VanderWolfImages), 122 (Gordzam), (Refal Schab), 152 (Meoita), 154 & 156 (Artyomanikeev), 158 (Olonho), 160 (Ra3rn), 162 (Coprid), 164 (Sashashukin), 167 (Zjm7100), 172 (Illuminativisual), 174 (Ryan Fletcher), 175 (Jozsef Soos), 180 (Gordzam), 182 (Ryan Fletcher), 184 (Igot Dolgov), 196 (Diogo Queiroz), 197 (Alfonsofotografia), 200 (Artyomanikeev), 204 & 205 (Jozsef Soos)

Eurofighter: 32
Getty Images: 18 (NurPhoto), 23 (VCG), 74 (Mahmud Turkia/AFP), 90 (Goh Chai Hin/AFP), 92 (AFP), 96 (Bloomberg), 97 (Universal Images Group), 126 & 128 (VCG), 129 (Future Publishing), 212 (Aamir Qureshi/AFP), 214 (VCG)

Lockheed Martin: 54 (Michael Jackson), 207

Public Domain: 22, 102, 203

David Raykovitz: 38

Saab: 88

Shutterstock: 20 (Samuel Lam), 84 & 85 (viper-zero), 106 (Fasttailwind), 130 (JetKat), 166 & 168 (Fasttailwind), 170 (Ryan Fletcher), 218 (EarnestTse), 219 (moh_bagusov2)

U.S. Air Force: 6 (MSGT John R Nimmo, Sr), 9 (2nd Lt Sam Eckholm), 24 (SSGT Marvin D Lynchard), 28 (SSGT Aaron Allmon), 34 (A1C Caleb Worpel), 36 (A1C Harry Brexel), 40 (TSGT Rob Tabor), 50 (A1C Erin Baxter), 52 (Capt Kip Sumner), 60 (SSGT William Rio Rosado), 66, 76 (MSGT John E Lasky), 100 (A1C Stephanie Rubi), 108 (A1C Albert Morel), 118 (SSGT John Rohrer), 124 (SrA Devlin Bishop), 134 (SSGT Derrick C Goode), 144 (TSGT Mike Buytas), 186 (TSGT Marlin G Zimmerman), 188 (Heide Couch), 190 (William R Lewis), 191 (SSGT Michael Battles), 193 (TSGT H H Deffner), 202 (A1C Erin V Currie), 208 (Heide Couch), 210 (William Lewis)

U.S. Air National Guard: 56 (MSGT Vincent De Groo), 70 & 71 (John Hughel), 58, 68 (SSGT Tony R. Tolley), 194 (TSGT Victoria Nelson)

U.S. Army: 206 (VIS Jason Johnston), 209 (TSGT Lou Hernandez)

U.S. Department of Defense: 138, 140 (Corporal Bryan Carter), 142

U.S. Navy: 62 (MCS Ryan U Kledzik), 64 (MCS3 Dustin Knight), 116 (MCS2 Gulianna Dunn), 136 (MCS2 John Herman), 192 (Lt Peter Scheu), 198 (MCS3 Elliot Schaudt)